SCALE MILITA
VEHICLE CONVERS

Dedication

To Jackie, without whom nothing would be possible.

SCALE MILITARY VEHICLE CONVERSIONS

DUNCAN HOWARTH

THE CROWOOD PRESS

First published in 2007 by
The Crowood Press Ltd
Ramsbury, Marlborough
Wiltshire SN8 2HR

www.crowood.com

British Library Cataloguing-in-Publication Data
A catalogue record for this book is available from the British Library.

ISBN   978 1 86126 888 4

Text, photography and all illustrations by Duncan Howarth.
Edited by Rachael Howarth.
Additional photography by Christian Howarth.

Photograph previous page: KV3 rear left flank.

Typeset and designed by D & N Publishing
Lambourn Woodlands, Hungerford, Berkshire.

Printed and bound in Singapore by Craft Print International.

Contents

Acknowledgements

During the preparation of this book many people have provided me with help, both materially and in the way of encouragement: Ian Young, Editor of *Military Machines International*, and Mark Askew, Editor of *Jeep World Magazine* for the provision of invaluable photographic material. Des, Alex and all of the crew at Modelzone, Manchester, for their encouragement. James Waters for his patient computer work and procurement of weapons. Terry at Cast-off for the FAMO wheels. My very good friend Tony Barber for his limitless help, and without whom my skills, such as they are, would have been much less. My daughter, Rachael Howarth, for a Herculean typing and editing effort. My son, Christian Howarth for all finished vehicle photography, in effect, qualifying the whole book.

Inspiration to persevere throughout the years has come from the incredible works of Alec Gee, Norman Abbey, Julian Benassi and latterly from Marcus Nicholls, Raul Garcia Latorre, and above all Gary Norris who was brave enough to give me my first writing break in *Military Modelcraft* magazine, and without whom this book would not have been possible.

Introduction – Tools and Techniques

Military hardware has been converted by the men of mechanized armies since wheeled and tracked vehicles first traversed the world's battlefields. Even though the model making industry worldwide has produced a vast range of types and sub-types of almost every vehicle ever conceived there are still, and will remain, significant gaps in their output. Model companies are hampered by

Fig. 1 *Frog and Airfix – giants of the 1960s.*

Fig. 2 *Magazines to be seen with in the 1970s, along with 'Oxford Bags' and platform shoes!*

budgetary and marketing constraints. These often dictate the production standardization of individual groups of models, such as variants of the Panther and Tiger, and the shape and structure of their catalogue ranges. This gives kit-bashers the world over the chance to have an adventure, and to produce a truly unique model of their own choice.

My model making journey began in 1964 when I was five years old and 'Sugar Puffs' cereal was giving away ten-piece, 1/72 scale kits of Ford Corsairs, MGBs and a Triumph Herald soft-top. Strange to think of them now as 'classic' cars when they were then so modern!

Throughout the 1960s and 1970s Airfix, Frog, Aurora, Pyro and others developed the kit-

building hobby incredibly quickly, with new models becoming available seemingly by the week (Fig. 1). By 1969 I had built enough Hurricanes and Bf 109s, so I attempted the Airfix military vehicle range. It struck me, when my favourite uncle bought me the Airfix Crusader tank, that there were quite a few variations of this vehicle built during World War Two and they were all there in *Airfix magazine* (Fig. 2). Thinking in an eleven-year-old's economics, the kit came with two turrets – Marks 1 and 2 – so just for when I got bored with them, I bought a sheet of 20 thou plasticard (cost: 2 shillings and 4 pence, or 12p in today's money). I then stretched some sprue and built myself an approximation of the Crusader anti-aircraft tank. After converting the Airfix

Fig. 3 *At top, the 1974-vintage Tamiya Jagdtiger alongside the brand new (and longer) DML version.*

Scammell tank transporter into an artillery tractor, I was completely hooked.

The 1970s brought a change in scale, and in manufacturers. One of my teachers at grammar school had bought a Datsun Cherry. A nice car, but it didn't last very long! When Tamiya set up shop, everyone expected, well, very little. A friend of mine bought their first Kübelwagen kit on the same weekend that I bought the Airfix 54mm 11th Hussar model. A week later, during my first attempt to attach its 5 thou plastic cross straps and stirrups, my mate turned up with his completed Kübel. We were both a bit gobsmacked: my Hussar had cost 3/6d (17.5p) whereas the Kübel was 13 shillings (65p) and worth every penny. I had heard the rumour that Tamiya had designed their kits originally to be compatible with the world standard of 1/32, or 54mm, scale model soldiers. Due to the plastic contracting on leaving the mould their Panther tank shrank to 1/35 scale, and they never looked back! In all but model soldier circles, 1/32nd scale military vehicle kits are all but forgotten (Fig. 3).

Throughout the 1990s, and into the new millennium, the hobby of military modelling and conversions has changed radically. After-market products, particularly in resin and etched brass, have presented new opportunities and challenges to modellers, while radical surgery with plastic sheet and rod has seemed less necessary to produce an original and exciting model.

There are still a good many vehicles that have not been produced as kits in any scale, and remain unlikely to be. In conversion and completely scratch-built model projects, there is no reason why etched brass and resin components cannot be used along with plastic parts – sheet, rod and strip – to produce vehicles varying widely in complexity, size and mass appeal.

The Hetzer *Flammpanzer* is a great place to start, needing outwardly only a new flame projector in place of the model's original main armament. At the other end of the scale, the Vomag with its 88mm Flak gun has an almost completely scratch-built body, chassis and running gear mated to an excellent replica of the legendary '88'. Step-by-step instructions are provided to research, plan and execute the models herein. They will hopefully inspire you to seek out more of this 'undiscovered country', which amounts to a hobby within a hobby, and a source of endless fascination.

CHAPTER 1

Getting Started

RESEARCH

The internet is an incredible source of information for modellers and kit converters alike. On the web you will find all manner of previously unseen material from all corners of the globe. However, caveat emptor – 'buyer beware'! Information found on the web should always be double-checked, as with any research. Websites are produced by human beings, and while the vast majority of the information will be of the highest quality, there will inevitably be some inaccuracies and omissions.

The military history and modelling communities are now better catered for, in publishing terms, than ever before. The wealth of well-researched material produced in Great Britain, America, and Europe has now been enhanced by previously unseen material from behind the former Iron Curtain. Publishers like Crowood, Ian Allan, Osprey, and Arms and Armour have produced a stream of quite remarkable books, spanning all aspects of the military world from all ages.

Magazines like *Military Modelling* and *Model Military International*, along with many of the foreign modelling magazines, are usually the first

Fig. 1.1 *MG 42 and Kar 98k, from the collection of Mr James Waters, make excellent reference.*

Fig. 1.2 *Archive photographs like this one are invaluable – wherever you come by them.*

stop for the conversion researcher. They are accompanied on the news-stands by *Military Machines* and *Classic Military Vehicles* magazines, which not only contain masses of beautifully reproduced contemporary photographs of preserved military vehicles, but a pleasing quantity of official and unofficial period photographs, some of which are very obscure indeed.

Local military vehicle trust groups are often well worth a visit. Along with the mass of meetings and rallies that they attend, such as Beltring in Kent and the 'Yanks' extravaganza at Uppermill, Lancashire in August each year, these enthusiasts are often seen in monthly battle re-enactments all over England and also in Europe and the USA. With a little diplomacy, you will find these multi-skilled individuals are often only too eager to let you photograph and measure the most 'intimate' parts of their military vehicles. For example, I am indebted to James Waters for the loan of his MG 42 and Kar 98k (Fig. 1.1) to use as modelling references. However, don't forget that to the lender, their vehicles are their models, so treat them as you would your own.

Often overlooked are family photographic archives (Fig. 1.2), which are invaluable for vehicle and figure research. An erstwhile neighbour of mine had some excellent material from when he was in Malaya during the Emergency there: he let me copy his photos of Canadian Otter armoured cars and SAS teams. Be prepared also for some disappointments: I used to work with an old German gentleman who was on the last half-track out of Kiev in late 1943, but unfortunately his album had been stolen in a recent burglary!

There are also many regimental museums throughout the country. As well as providing invaluable help in the local community, the Lancashire Fusiliers in Bury have an extensive archive, which they are more than willing to let you use (Fig. 1.3). Their new premises promise even more information at the public's fingertips when complete.

The Royal Armoured Corps museum at Bovington in Dorset is an exceptional resource. There is a bewildering assortment of vehicles for you to photograph and measure, along with an excellent photographic archive. In France the

Fig. 1.3 *Lancashire Fusiliers mount-up on mainland China.*

Fig. 1.4 *Dodge 6 × 6 at the 'Yanks' weekend, Uppermill, Lancashire.*

Saumur Armour Museum and in the USA the Aberdeen Proving Ground are just two of the many resources you could exploit while on family holidays (Fig. 1.4). If you are a little adventurous and would like to see Porsche's Tiger *Maus*, the *Karl* tracked mortar and hundreds of other very obscure vehicles, try Moscow's Kubinka Tank Museum. Even in the depths of winter, this is an extraordinary place. Details for these and many more establishments with extensive vehicle collections can be found on the internet.

When all else fails, try the scrapyards. Several years ago in a Bolton yard I found two Scammell Commanders, a 1942 Fordson and 1943 Bedford QL command vehicle. The latter provided the basis for plans and the subsequent conversion of an old Airfix/Max QL kit into a radar command vehicle.

Finally, the *Military Modelling* magazine plans service is an excellent resource. For further details, pick up the magazine or cruise the website.

TOOLS AND TECHNIQUES

Conversion work, for the most part, is a precision business. As a consequence, it is always best to buy the best possible equipment that you (or your parents) can afford. Having said that, a craft knife and a metal ruler imported from China will often do the job as well as a Swann-Morton scalpel and a ruler by Stanley or similar (Figs 1.5 and 1.6). A lot will boil down to what suits the individual and their pocket.

Whichever knife you choose, always take great care with it and where possible cut with a metal edge between you and the blade: back in the 1960s my father inadvertently removed his left middle finger while using the blade from a wood-plane as an impromptu chisel! Needless to say the language that ensued was more than colourful. Combination rulers in plastic with a metal straight edge are an excellent option, as some now have an anti-slip styrene foam pad on

Fig. 1.5 *Essential tools –*
scalpel, blades and good
scissors.

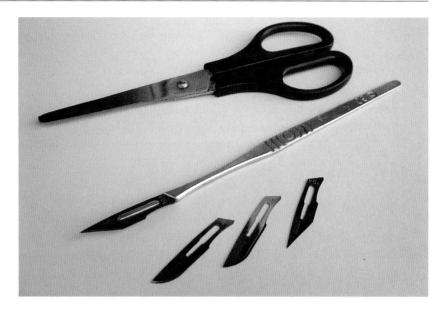

one side – very useful when working with any type of plastic.

Scissors are often useful for rough-cutting larger pieces of sheet into useable sizes. Wahl and similar German products are crafted from Solingen steel. However, I recently found a pack of three different-sized scissors at my local Ikea.

They are among the finest I have ever used, so always keep your eyes peeled.

Several saws will also be of use for plastic of 60 thou and thicker (Fig. 1.7), as well as various gauges of tube, metal and resin components. A small coping saw is a good place to start – X-Acto in the USA produce these, along with a very

Fig. 1.6 *The centre ruler*
was used by my uncle,
who helped build
Lancasters during World
War Two.

15

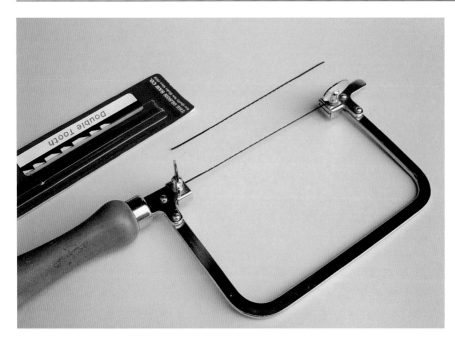

Fig. 1.7 *Jigsaw and a variety of blades.*

diverse range of modelling tools and implements. A jigsaw, when used with care (and with a good, taut blade), will make very short work of casting blocks on larger resin components such as wheels and tyres. A set of good compasses will prove useful (Fig. 1.8). My expensive Rotring multi-pen compass served well for thirty years before it died recently. I bought an excellent replacement from W.H. Smith: it will fit any pen or pencil, and was extraordinarily cost-effective. I shall be interested to see whether or not it lasts another thirty years!

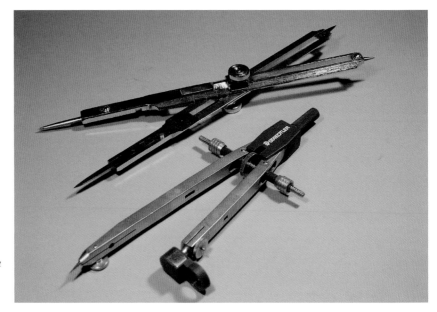

Fig. 1.8 *First-rate German compasses, and a real rarity – proportional scaling dividers.*

Fig. 1.9 *Compasses and circle-cutters.*

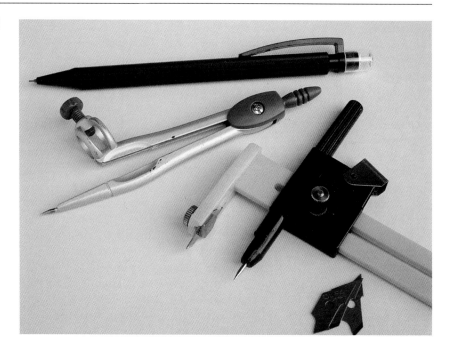

A compass cutter is a must for the multiplicity of discs you will cut (Fig. 1.9). However, be very careful if you use a plastic one: if you press too hard the frame will distort, giving a misshapen, semi-elliptical cut. Bearing this in mind, always make sure you keep the point of the compass cutter pressed hard into its centre point, while keeping your fingers at a safe distance!

A vice is any modeller's, or indeed engineer's, third hand. There are now a good many custom-made model makers' vices, and if you are stuck for space most of them are fitted with screw clamps

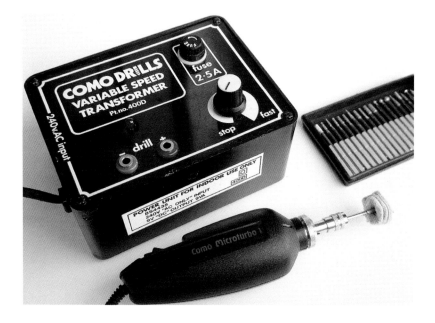

Fig. 1.10 *High-speed (variable) miniature drill.*

17

underneath so that you can move them quickly if the in-laws are coming around for tea. They last a long time, too: I use a model engineer's vice that belonged to my grandfather, who bought it in 1929 for 3d (1.5p) – and it was made in England! 'G' clamps are also a handy back-up tool, but remember to shield the jaws from soft plastic surfaces (most usually with other bits of soft plastic).

Multi-purpose power tools from Dremel or Minicraft (Fig. 1.10) are very useful for everything, from drilling simple holes to adding realistic textures to rough-cast armour plate on turret sides.

There is a wealth of these tools (and engraving tools for detail carving) around, but just as interesting are the miniature milling machines, post drills, vertical milling machine, and so on. These can all be used on plastic, but come into their own when gun barrels need to be turned, and holes drilled into the side of brass rod or tube.

Modellers vary in the painting methods and finishes they prefer, but the airbrush is still the weapon of choice for anyone serious about model finishing (Figs 1.11–1.14). As well as giving an overall finish to a model, they can be used to replicate camouflage schemes, and thereafter to apply successive thinned coats of paint, or 'filters', to replicate weathering and decay of paint and metal surfaces. Always keep your eyes open for interestingly rusted surfaces for reference. Good quality paint brushes are also critical to a good finished

product – Winsor and Newton, or Vallejo are recommended (Fig. 1.15).

Side-cup, gravity-feed and suction-feed airbrushes are not difficult to acquire from any model or hobby shop. They all follow the basic premise of the original 'Aerograph', now manufactured by DeVilbiss: a stream of finely controlled air over a needle, atomizing a gentle flow of paint or ink. Once mastered, this is an invaluable tool, but *you* must control *it*, not the other way around. Also, don't spray any paint or solvent without ample ventilation, a mask and eye protection. Be prepared to build up your base colour in three to five thinned coats of paint.

Conversely, you can use any of the excellent aerosols now produced by Tamiya, Humbrol (Fig. 1.16) and the like. After thoroughly shaking the can, it is best to give the model a light 'dust' coating, letting it dry thoroughly before applying a heavier coat and, if necessary, one more lighter one. Even though their nozzles are mass produced, these aerosols are excellent, provided of course that the paint is thoroughly mixed first. One more useful addition to the aerosol armoury is a little attachment called the can-gun. This adds nothing to the can's performance, but makes it a jolly site less painful on the index finger! You will also need a wide variety of enamels, acrylics and oil paints (Fig. 1.17).

Fig. 1.11 *Beautiful Iwata airbrush kit.*

Fig. 1.12 *DeVilbiss 'Super 63' and venerable Aerograph 'retoucher'.*

Fig. 1.13 *Outstanding 'Badger' 200, a subtle, yet hardy airbrush.*

Fig. 1.14 *Propellant, cleaner, valves and air-traps are all invaluable accessories.*

Fig. 1.15 *Always buy the best paint brushes that you can afford – and look after them.*

Fig. 1.16 *Spray-paints, and CFC- free cyano activator.*

Rivets are a common feature, particularly on the earlier armoured vehicles produced when welded construction was less common. The new rivet-maker implement, available from Historex Agents of Dover, is invaluable for producing perfectly uniform plastic rivet heads in a variety of sizes. All you have to do is apply them using the point of a new scalpel blade. Otherwise you can backtrack and fabricate each rivet head from tiny portions of plastic rod, using ultra fine wet and dry paper to dome the heads – have fun with that!

Revell and Humbrol now make an excellent range of polystyrene glues (Fig. 1.18) and, more importantly, dispensers. Since the old days when Airfix glue was only available in tubes with, I suspect, a high lead content, things have improved. The needle nozzles available from most manufacturers allow delivery of a much more measured dose. Superglue (cyanoacrylate adhesive) for resin, and indeed metal, is now available in a variety of consistencies and strengths. The aerosol activator rapidly accelerates its drying process to a few short seconds, so be prepared. As always – ventilate.

19

Fig. 1.17 *Paint, coloured pencils and pastels all help the finished model seem more realistic.*

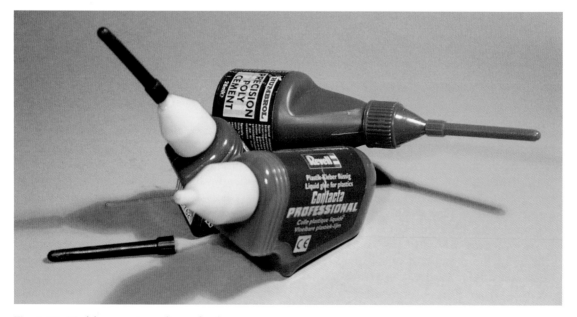

Fig. 1.18 *Model cement in applicator bottles.*

FORMING AND SHAPING

Injection moulding, vacuum forming and resin casting are three of the cornerstones of model kit production. Fabrication from plastic sheet has been made much easier in the recent past, not only due to the vast range of thicknesses of sheet now available (from 5 thou to 100 thou nominally). From Slaters and Evergreen in the USA there is now a huge range of rods, tubes and strips in everything from flat, 1mm wide, 5 thou section, to huge I- and L-section beams. Plastruct also make a tremendous range of plastic rods, and some rather elaborate trellis and bridging sections. Due to the nature of construction of the full-sized vehicles we are replicating, you will find that the vast majority of components can be fabricated from plastic sheet, rod and strip/angle.

When cutting the sheet with a scalpel, take care to keep the metal ruler or try-square (Fig. 1.19) between yourself and the blade. After cutting the sheet, one edge will often have a slightly raised portion along its edge: this can be removed by careful sanding with very fine 'wet and dry' paper, or scraping the scalpel's blade along the edge of the plastic, sloping it away from you at about 45 degrees ('paring'). After two or three passes, check the cut edge with your finger. Cutting a radius on the corner of the sheet is best done using an architect's radius curve – the metal ones are still available. You can of course cut them by eye, after marking them with a pencil. Any irregularities can always be removed with wet and dry paper.

Holes are always best drilled carefully and slowly, with the subject to be bored safely clamped – whether you are using a post drill, or a hand-held Dremel or similar. To avoid cracking the edge of the plastic around the hole, try putting a tiny blob of washing-up liquid on the end of the drill bit. This eases its passage by reducing the friction between the two surfaces, but be sure to wash it thoroughly with water as washing-up liquid and enamel paint most definitely do not mix.

Some smaller holes can be easily opened up with the point of a scalpel blade. A very slim handle is best for this (such as a Swann-Morton No. 7), the slender centre portion being easily rolled back and forth between thumb and forefinger. Choose a 10A or 11 blade.

A chamfered edge on, say, 60 thou sheet is easily achieved by using one of the commercially available sanding blocks, carefully held at the correct angle. Alternatively, a small block of wood wrapped in fine abrasive paper will do.

A Dremel, Minicraft or similar drill can be easily used on plastic or resin, along with a suitable abrasive bit to add a realistic texture to armour-plate surfaces. Always make sure you have your reference for each process close at hand throughout the job.

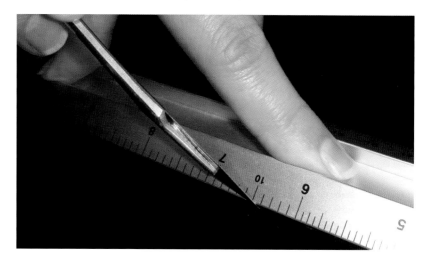

Fig. 1.19 *Take care when cutting with a knife against a ruler's edge.*

CHAPTER 2

Hetzer *Flammpanzer* 38(t)

In order for the Germans to even consider using their blitzkrieg tactics in Europe in 1939, they first needed to seize Czechoslovakia and its burgeoning arms industries; this they did in 1938. Foremost amongst the Czech arms works was Ceskosmoravska Kolben Danek of Prague. Their CKD 38t was to become the basis of a huge number of German assault guns and flak vehicles, and the 'Hetzer' tank destroyer. Twenty of these were converted to carry the *Flammenwerfer* 41 flamethrower unit in 1944 at the express request of Hitler – though at a time when the Germans needed to destroy as many Allied tanks as possible, such terror weapons should arguably have stayed at the back of the queue. The 14mm-calibre flame projector carried 265gal (1,200ltr) of fuel and propellant: enough for twenty-four flame bursts of four seconds' duration each.

The Tamiya Hetzer Tank Destroyer (*Jagdpanzer*) kit in 1/48 scale is state of the art. The moulding is crisp, clean and consistent throughout the build, with link and length tracks to finish. The only questionable part of the build is the hull bottom, which is cast in zinc alloy. This adds nothing to the model's accuracy or look, and actually precludes the modeller from some future conversion potential. Perhaps after-market companies can rectify this state of affairs.

CONSTRUCTION

This conversion is by far the easiest of our selection, but requires no less care and attention to detail.

The parts review is, for the most part, quite excellent. The chassis, lower hull and running gear go together easily, even bearing in mind that all of the components outlined in section 4 of the instruction sheet need to be affixed to the lower hull by means of superglue cyanoacrylate adhesive. The curing time of this glue can be artificially speeded up by the use of an accelerator or 'activator'; I use the CFC-free version from Rite-Lok, but any of the commercially available versions will reduce the setting time of superglue to three or four seconds. Be careful, wear at least a paper industrial mask for protection and open the windows.

Once the lower hull and running gear are assembled (Fig. 2.1), check that the wheels are square to the body and the vertical; the link and length tracks can now be assembled onto the wheels (Fig. 2.2). This process is much easier than it used to be, helped in no small part by the accuracy and crispness of the moulding in this kit. Follow the kit instructions closely and make sure

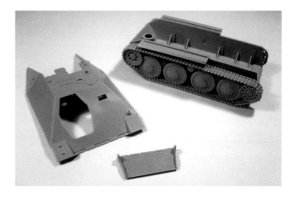

Fig. 2.1 *Hetzer chassis and hull sub-assemblies need model cement and cyano adhesive.*

Fig. 2.2 *Metal lower hull detail. Make sure that wheels are square to the ground and hull sides.*

that the tracks run in the correct direction. This can be checked with the box art if you have no clear pictures to hand.

By stage 8 you will be on to the upper hull assembly. Complete the whole according to the kit instructions, missing off the gun and 'gun barrel base' assembly from sections 9 and 10, plus any potentially fragile components from the upper hull and rear. Please note that at this stage it is preferable that upper and lower hull assemblies are kept separate.

Referring to the in-build photographs throughout the next sequence, first trim out the portion

shown from the gun barrel base (B42). This will then appear as a 'horse shoe' shape (Fig. 2.3) which, with careful trimming, will accommodate the single template on the plans/elevations provided. Cut this from 20 thou plastic sheet and insert carefully, before sanding and blending into the gun barrel base (Fig. 2.7).

The pictures on page 23–24 (Figs 2.4–2.8) show the mounting components from section 9 of the kit instructions, which should then have the gun barrel location pin reduced to about 2mm in length, the assembly being inserted

Fig. 2.3 *Cut to this line to make aperture flat in section.*

Fig. 2.4 *Main armament ball-mount before spigot is trimmed.*

Fig. 2.5 *Correct aperture profile.*

Fig. 2.6 *Main armament spigot trimmed to length.*

Fig. 2.7 *Template blank in place before hole is 'slotted'.*

Fig. 2.8 *Discard the kit's main armament.*

(without glue) into the gun barrel base. The *Saukopf* or pig's head mantlet (part B40) is not used, nor is the gun barrel (part B9). They are replaced by a 32mm length cut from the muzzle end of a 1/35 scale Sherman's 75mm gun, and a bucket! The latter is taken from the Tamiya 1/48 scale accessory set, which also includes fuel drums, jerrycans and the canvas storage rolls used on the model's rear engine decking.

Carefully trim the bucket's bottom rim flush with its base and use an emery paper until square. Do the same with the gun barrel, being careful to open out the muzzle with a craft knife to accommodate part B8 from the Hetzer kit. Also, bear in mind that the barrel is actually a thin cylindrical sleeve that protects the *Flammenwerfer* from shell fragments and small arms fire. Then make a tubular (2mm) spigot that will marry the 'bucket' end of the projector to the gun mounting by protruding through the slotted hole in the previously mounted template. Fig. 2.9 shows the finished assembly.

The complete assembly should then be allowed to dry thoroughly before being mated to the front of the upper hull, which will then be affixed to the lower hull assembly, taking care that all joints are superglued to ensure a strong, immediate bond. The wide-angle episcope atop the gun barrel base should then be cut from plastic sheet (60 thou). It measures 6 × 2 × 3mm and glues in place as shown in the plan drawings.

When the hull is assembled completely, add the *Schurzen*, or side skirts. These are perfectly acceptable components (B20 and B21) but if, as I did, you wish to remove one of the centre sections, you will need to pare down the resulting intermediate edges to resemble scale thickness, as these parts are almost 1mm thick.

After-market products in etched brass may be preferable to replace the kit parts. When a shield is removed, remember to make the joint between the upper hull sponson and the lower hull 'ledge' solid and filled. The extra stowage on the engine decking was taken from the excellent Tamiya accessories set; in addition Tamiya – and others – now manufacture an extensive range of model figures, including German tank/self-propelled gun crews and infantry.

Fig. 2.9 *Note 2mm tube protruding from barrel sleeve's end.*

Fig. 2.10 *When positioning stowage, always refer to reference shots of actual vehicles where possible.*

Fig. 2.11 *Camouflage in progress; take care to mask exhaust when painting.*

Fig. 2.12 *Flamethrower outer sleeve in place (76mm, 1/35th scale Sherman barrel-end).*

PAINTING AND COMPLETION

After two coats of Tamiya mid-sand from one of their extremely fine aerosols, a 'shadowing' tone of sand/dark earth was applied sparingly (Fig. 2.10). Mid-green and rust-brown were then applied with a number 4 sable brush, lifting the brush point gradually throughout each stroke to replicate this late-war tank hunter camouflage, running at 45 degrees across the whole vehicle, including the wheels (Fig. 2.11). German wartime camouflage colours were a synthetic concoction, specifically manufactured to be diluted by virtually any non-corrosive liquid, including water, petrol and –

indeed – urine. The dilution and substance used would both dictate, along with natural weathering, the exact colours and tones. Intelligent commanders would take this into account, along with the prevalent topography and light conditions when applying colours in the field.

Mig powders (from the very inventive Miguel Jiminez company) were dusted onto the wheels on top of a mid-sand dry-brush paint coat (Fig. 2.12). The exhaust was also given the treatment, with the powders being mixed into a suitable rust shade and dabbed carefully into place.

In all, a great place to start converting military models, with a kit that is pre-eminent in its field.

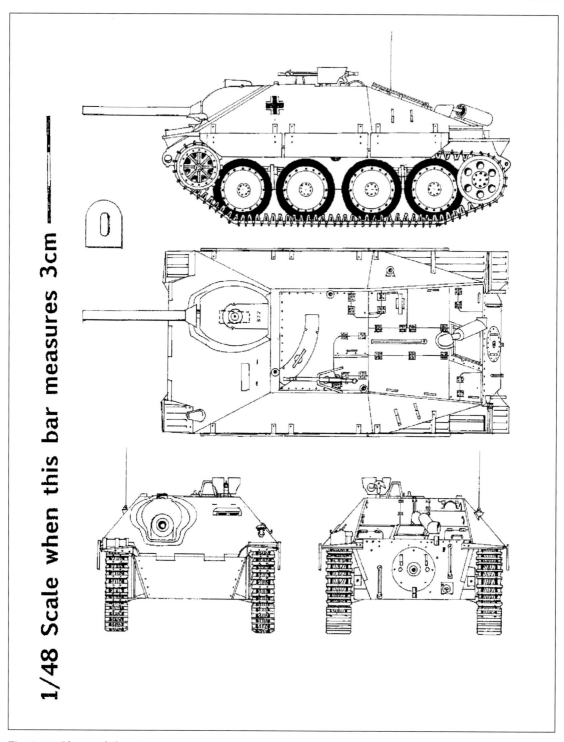

1/48 Scale when this bar measures 3cm

Fig. 2.13 *Plans and elevations.*

Fig. 2.14 *Reference shots – 'ambush' camouflage* circa *1944–5.*

CHAPTER 3

Ford of Canada
F30s Ambulance

South Africa's war began soon after Great Britain's. The first South African division drove the 3,000+ miles from the Transvaal to Libya in North Africa, taking thousands of men to fight the Italians in Abyssinia along the way. After distinguishing themselves in bitter hand-to-hand battles, from El Alamein to Tobruk, the 'fighting Springboks' reformed into the 6th South African division in time for their landing in Italy in early 1943.

Major General Evered Poole CB DSO, the popular GOC of 6th SA Division, decided to re-equip with the very best weapons and equipment available to these eager Commonwealth 'scrappers'. New Shermans and 5½in howitzers were supported by a fantastic array of half-tracks and trucks. Ford and Chevrolet of Canada provided many of these trucks in the form of troop carriers, workshop vehicles, field artillery tractors (Quads) and, of course, ambulances.

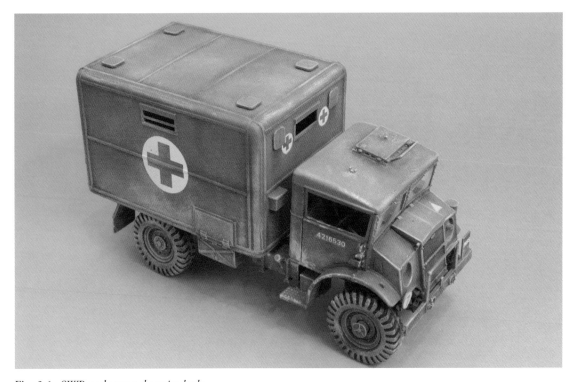

Fig. 3.1 *SWB early general service body.*

The Ford C29QF/F30 ambulance was a triumph of functional design. It was produced by Ford, with cab numbers 12 and 13 (our vehicle) to carry four stretchers in an all-steel panelled box body, with very large double rear doors. With their four-speed gearbox, hydraulic brakes and leaf-spring suspension, the F30s and F60s were a revelation to their drivers, and a godsend to the injured occupants, being both fast and fairly comfortable.

The Italeri 1/35th scale Quad CMP kit is now venerable, to say the least. I remember it from the 1970s in the UK, initially as a Max kit, then IMAI, then Airfix and – most recently – Italeri. And thank goodness! Allied soft-skins are still thin on the ground, all these years after the war. This model still holds its own against much younger competition and is still widely available,

cheap and a real gift to conversion fans. Refer to the relevant photographs and plans/exploded views as you proceed: this conversion is actually much easier than it looks.

CONSTRUCTION

First in the 'chop-shop' is the chassis (part 1a). Referring to the photograph (Fig. 3.2), carefully chop the chassis side-rails midway between the rear spring hanger bracket and the transfer box (part 4a). Insert two 24mm lengths of suitable section 'Evergreen' plastic strip, cementing the whole assembly on a flat surface to maintain the squareness and integrity of the finished component. Then add the extra cross member as shown.

Figs 3.2–3.5 *(clockwise from top left) 2. chassis make-up pieces; 3. rear door windows; 4. disposition of vents; 5. side glazing and rear door handles.*

Figs 3.6–3.9 *(clockwise from top left) 6. prop-shaft position; 7. under-body panniers in place; 8. cab and chassis must be square, one to the other; 9. hinge positions to rear door.*

Proceed with the rest of the chassis and running gear as per the kit instructions; however, you will need to extend (Fig. 3.6) the rear prop shaft (part 26a). Chop out the thick, tubular section, leaving the universal (Hardy-Spicer) joints in place in the transfer box and rear differential (part 28a). Add a 35mm length of suitable plastic tube and leave to set. When the vehicle chassis and running gear are complete, lady luck will lend a hand. The field artillery tractor body is redundant. However, the complete cab from the 15cwt truck variant is included in this kit. This is a 'mini-kit' in its own right and requires a great deal of care to ensure the correct alignment of body panels, doors, mudguards and roof. Considering this kit is forty years old in design, a little patience will pay dividends.

Referring to the template and exploded diagram, start by cutting the floor from 40 thou plastic card, taking care to cut the wheel arch recesses exactly square and the floor corners with a 4mm radius. The four corner uprights and roof support framework can be fabricated from Plastruct tubing or from square-section strip that can be radiused with fine emery paper upon completion of the structure. Then add the body side and end panels, along with the roof (Figs 3.3 and 3.4), as per the illustrations, being sure to check the squareness at each stage. Needless to say, if the rear doors are left open, an interior will need to be researched and added. Four stretchers in two-deep banks at each side were carried, with the top two being wound up and down on a

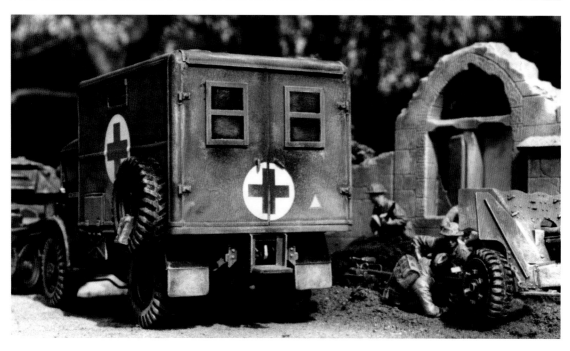

ABOVE: Fig 3.10 *Anti-tank team in trouble – note position of rear step.* BELOW: Fig 3.11 *Painted and weathered.*

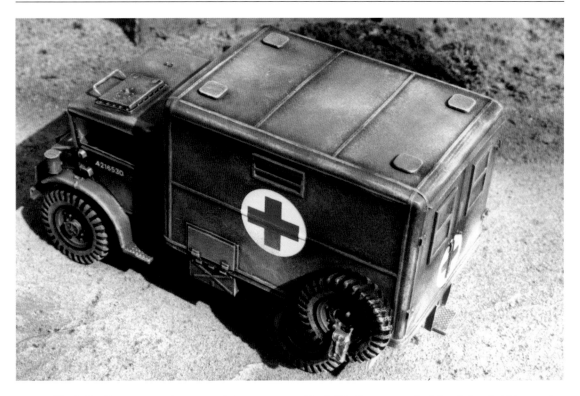

ABOVE: Fig 3.12 *Crew stowage kept to a minimum.* BELOW: Fig 3.13 *Rear spare wheel fitted, South African style.*

Fig. 3.14 *Heavy general service body with late pattern cab (note circular hip-ring).*
BELOW: *Embossed logo detail.*

worm-geared crank mechanism. My reference was unreliable, so best of luck with that! Hopefully, more of these vehicles will have survived in the USA.

Very fine 'Evergreen' strip is then used to trim the window apertures at the side, front and rear, referring to the scale plans where necessary. The cabinets and panniers are likewise trimmed, and the catches and hinges carefully added from strip and rod. The rear door hinges are of the spiral 'rise and fall' self-closing type (Fig. 3.9) on some versions, and standard on other bodies. Door handles are from pared-down plastic rod. The vents are then added from 30 thou sheet to the top and body front, as per the diagrams (Fig. 3.7).

Finally, the whole body is trimmed with 2mm plastic strip as shown in the plans and elevations, then sanded carefully until the strips are almost flush with the body proper. The ambulance body is then attached to the chassis via three latitudinal transoms of 3mm thickness, cut from plastic strip to the ambulance body's width. Once in place, the rear step is added, bearing in mind that this rigid step is one of several types fitted. L-section plastic rod and the 'treadplate' step from the kit are used (Fig. 3.10).

PAINTING

Most Commonwealth forces used this vehicle during and after World War Two, so many colour combinations are possible. The colour scheme shown, light olive green, is typical of those seen on late-war vehicles, especially those of the 6th South African division during the Apennine mountains campaign and the drive on Rome. The scheme shown on the plans and elevations is a Tunisian campaign variation. Weathering is pretty much a free-for-all, as the extremes of weather conditions encountered in the Italian campaign were legendary. Firstly, I black-airbrushed the joints and shadows, before using a pale stone dry-brush coating (Fig. 3.11) to replicate the dust from months of campaigning. Coloured chalk then gave the latest coating of local mud and dust.

In conclusion, this is still a fine old kit and, with a little imagination, careful research and planning, can be converted into any one of thirty (or so) different vehicles, including articulated trailer-tractor units, gantry trucks and workshop vehicles.

Fig. 3.15 *Petrol filler spout detail (left), and side light detail with wiring (right).*

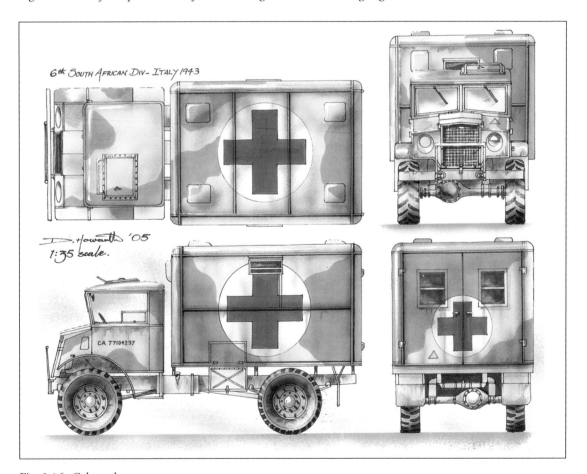

Fig. 3.16 *Colour plans.*

Fig. 3.17 *North-West Europe finish – Canadian Army.*

Fig. 3.18 *SWB early general service body.*

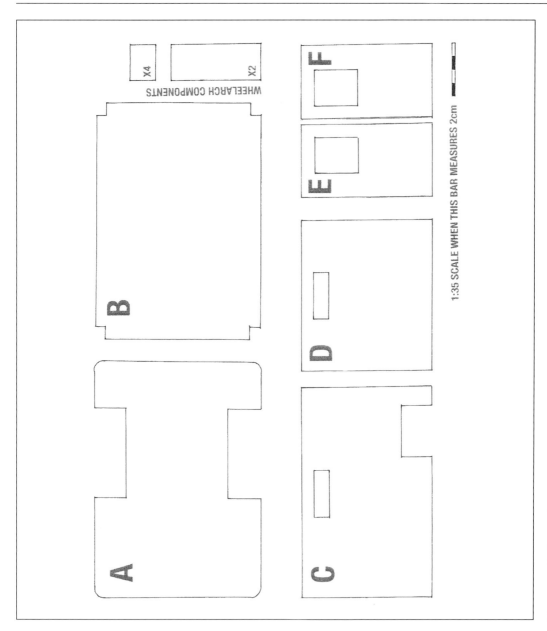

Fig. 3.19 *Body template.*

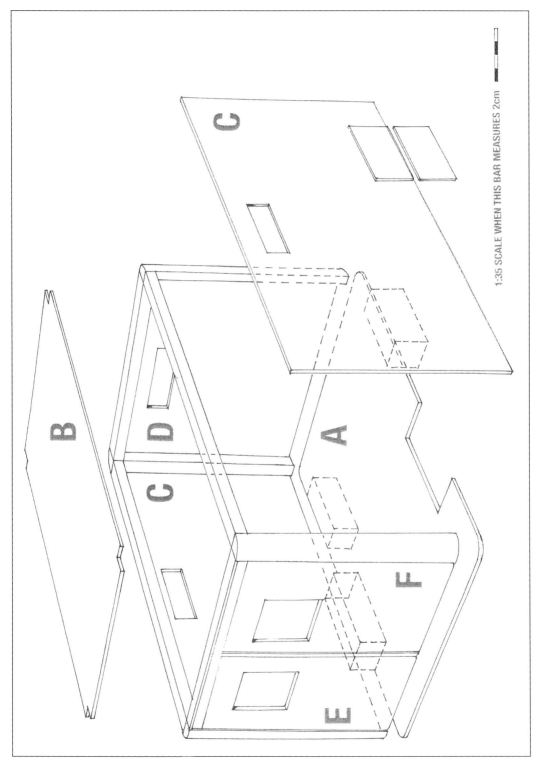

1:35 SCALE WHEN THIS BAR MEASURES 2cm

Fig. 3.20 *Exploded assembly diagram.*

CHAPTER 4

Jeep T27 Rocket Launcher

Rockets can have a devastating effect on an enemy's morale, and have been used since the time of Genghis Khan to obliterate armies, equipment and buildings in a relatively cost-effective way.

During the Allied army's advance across northwest Europe, softening up German positions while incurring the least casualties became a major concern. Along with the Sherman T34 Calliope system came a smaller cousin, the Jeep-mounted T27. It was built in relatively small numbers, in both eight- and twelve-barrelled versions. The electrically ignited rockets could be triggered from inside the armoured cab housing or – preferably – remotely by a 'Davies box' from a relatively safe distance, away from the incredible vacuum created by a rapid multiple launch.

Fig. 4.1 *Patrol in the Schwarzwald. Note igniter details.*

The Jeep's war-winning capabilities are very well documented. Interestingly, its legendary mobility was originally the result of mating together two rear axles from Austin Sevens.

Jeeps are very widely available to the modern-day modeller, in most scales. I chose the venerable Italeri Jeep because it is the only one now to come with a trailer, which is handy for carrying the launcher's ammunition. This old kit goes together very easily. However, you may encounter a little flash, especially on the more delicate parts. Careful trimming will pay dividends, and mould-line removal becomes easier with practice! The Tamiya Jeep would also be eminently suitable, although in its latest incarnation it lacks the trailer and accessories of the groundbreaking earlier kit.

GETTING STARTED

First, build the Jeep. If you do use the Italeri vehicle, trim off the jerrycan bracket locater and the angled wheel support bracket. Carefully sand the rear bulkhead of the Jeep until perfectly smooth. At this stage, reference should be made to the exploded diagram/templates, and the excellent wartime photographs reproduced here with the kind permission of Mark Askew of Jeep Books Ltd, an acknowledged expert in the field of US military vehicles.

The amount of detailing you do, particularly on the rocket tube igniters, is down to individual preference and the scale that you are working in. Hopefully, there is enough information here to provide a comprehensive overview.

The placing of template B is critical to the look of the finished vehicle. Cut it from 20 thou sheet and, after carefully squaring and dressing the edges, cement it vertically in the place indicated in the elevation drawing. With the driving compartment details installed, add the elevation cranking mechanism box and its accompanying handle, referring to Fig. 4.2 for its exact position. Add internal bracing strips to template B where shown.

Cut out template A from 20 thou sheet. Using the edge of a ruler and strong finger pressure, bend the component by 10 degrees along the

Fig. 4.2 *Templates A and B with bracing strips for strength.*

Fig. 4.3 *Side blast shields in place.*

Fig. 4.4 *Position of forward sliding blast-shield.*

dotted line, until the attitude shown in the drawings is achieved. Glue it into place (Fig. 4.3).

With the Jeep's kit windscreen fixed in place and mated to template A at the top (Fig. 4.4), blank the aperture with a 10 thou strip measuring 34 × 10mm with a 12 × 5mm aperture on the driver's side. Position the angle-iron rails on the outermost side, parallel to one another, 6mm apart. The sliding blanking piece for the window aperture should measure 6 × 10mm and fit snugly between the rails. The windscreen side blast protectors (two off, template E) should then be cemented into place as shown on the elevation drawing.

THE LAUNCH TUBES

Cut twelve-off launch tubes using template I, from 5mm outside diameter plastic tube (Figs 4.5 and 4.6). Alternatively, try brass tubing: it is of a thinner gauge and its use will obviate the need to bore out the ends of the tubes to a slightly larger diameter with a Dremel, as I did (Fig. 4.8).

Cement the tubes together side by side, in two banks of six (Fig. 4.7). When the assembly is dry, place it vertically down onto a small piece of very fine emery paper. Sand until the tube ends are all completely flush with one another and their surface is at 90 degrees to the tube sides. Repeat

Fig. 4.5 *Two banks, each of six tubes, before ends are levelled.*

Fig. 4.6 *Careful alignment is critical.*

Fig. 4.7 *Positioning igniter-caps in bored-out tube ends.*

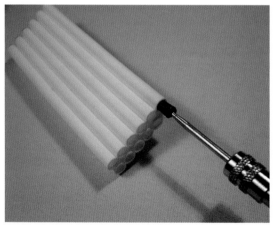

Fig. 4.8 *Use a carborundum 'burr' to hollow out the tube ends.*

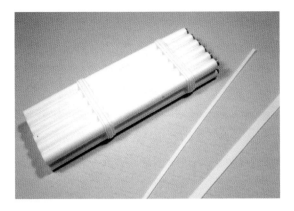

Fig. 4.9 *Templates J and K in forward and rear positions.*

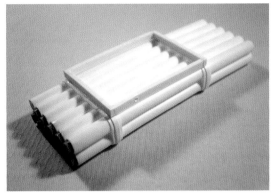

Fig. 4.10 *Template H in place. Note relation to retaining straps.*

the process at the other end. Add the details shown at AA using plastic strip and rod (Fig. 4.9). Each launch tube ignition assembly should measure 4 × 2.5mm wide when complete. My ignition caps at the base of the launch tubes came from the Academy 'Achilles' kit and are the bases from 17pdr artillery rounds. Alternatively, these components could quite easily be made from slices of sprue with sections cut from thin plastic rod for the centres. The wiring is up to you!

Cut two items of template J from 30 thou sheet. Wrap them around the tubes in the places shown in profile on the elevation drawing. Secure them with plastic cement, starting on the underside of the tubes. When dry, secure to the side and, when this is dry in turn, glue it to the top, then join to the other end underneath. Secure with masking tape. Repeat the process twice, wrapping two off template K (from 30 thou sheet) around the two J components (Fig. 4.10).

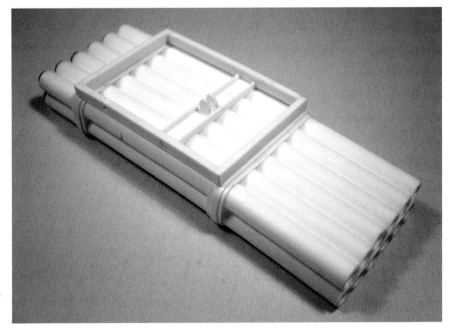

Fig. 4.11 *'U' section support for pinion rod top end bracket.*

Complete template H from 2 × 3mm plastic strip (rectangular section). Drill two 2mm holes using the Dremel or, preferably, an upright 'post' drill, toward the rear of each of the long sides of the tube's cradle.

Place a U-section bar, with two small brackets at its centre, beneath the cradle as shown in the photographs. This will be supported by the rod emerging from the top of the pinion box (F, G). The rear support rod is then located centrally, in the position shown by the photographs (Fig. 4.11).

The last pieces join the tripod launcher supports to the rear of template B – the cabin rear – and can be seen clearly in the wartime shots.

ROCKET LAUNCHER TRIPODS (×2)

With reference to the photographs, cut four off template C (from 30 thou sheet) and cement two on each side of the jeep's rear (Fig. 4.12), each forming an apex 26mm apart from each other. Cut two off template D, again from 1.5mm rod, and use them to complete each tripod support once the pivots (5 × 9mm each – Fig. 4.14) are in place at the top. Halfway down the tripod supports are two 2mm strip bracing-pieces (Fig. 4.13). Joining the two rearmost 'legs' are two L-angle support strips, across the rear of the vehicle. Their exact positions are shown in the rear elevation drawing.

Fig. 4.12 *Template C, four off in position.*

Fig. 4.13 *First bracing strips and 'L' section rear brace.*

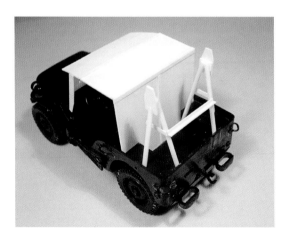

Fig. 4.14 *Hinge brackets minus pivot-bolt heads.*

Fig. 4.15 *Pinion elevation mechanism housing.*

Fig. 4.16 *Pinion elevating rod in position.*

Fig. 4.17 *Pinion rod elevating crank position.*

In between the rear supports, and attached to the rear (outer) face of template B, cement the rack, pinion box and the linkage (Fig. 4.15), which will locate in the bottom bracket beneath the launch tubes. The box is made from two off template G and one off template F (both from 30 thou sheet), the latter being kinked on the dotted line. A 3mm strip will close off the top of the box. From its top, my (elevation) adjuster rod measures 20mm (Fig. 4.16). This will vary, however, depending upon the degree of elevation required.

The paint job is north-west Europe and pretty stock (Fig. 4.19). The weathering is a little extreme (Figs 4.1 and 4.21) but, by the end of the war, 'environmental' camouflage was being liberally applied, even daubed all over vehicles, as men's desire to survive the war motivated them to disguise their vehicles more and more extremely.

Fig. 4.18 *Rocket tubes in position showing igniter brackets and clips.*

The interior should be fairly dirty also but, for dashboard details, see the interior shot of the real thing. Though spartan in the extreme, the Jeep's instruments should be carefully executed with the same 000 brush that you used to add the scratches to the paintwork.

As can be seen from the accompanying wartime pictures, there were at least two variants of this particular conversion, and I will be trying the eight-barrelled version on a metal 1/18th scale Jeep from one of the French manufacturers soon.

Fig. 4.19 *Two coats of base colour, with initial shading.*

Fig. 4.20 *Ensure that rocket-tubes are fixed at a convincing angle.*

Fig. 4.21 *On location in the woods. Watch for condensation on the camera lens.*

Fig. 4.22 *Wartime shots – loading rockets.*

Fig. 4.23 *Jeep trailer and dashboard details.*

Fig. 4.24 *Wartime shots, 12-barrelled and 8-barrelled versions.*

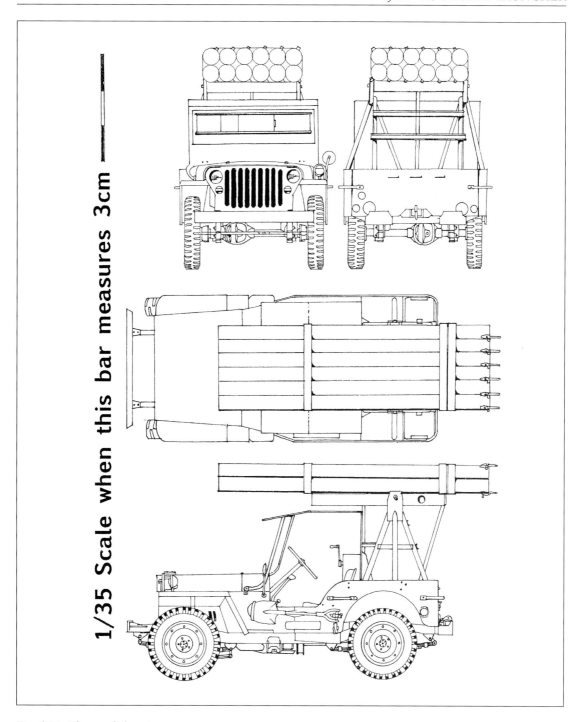

1/35 Scale when this bar measures 3cm

Fig. 4.25 *Plans and elevations.*

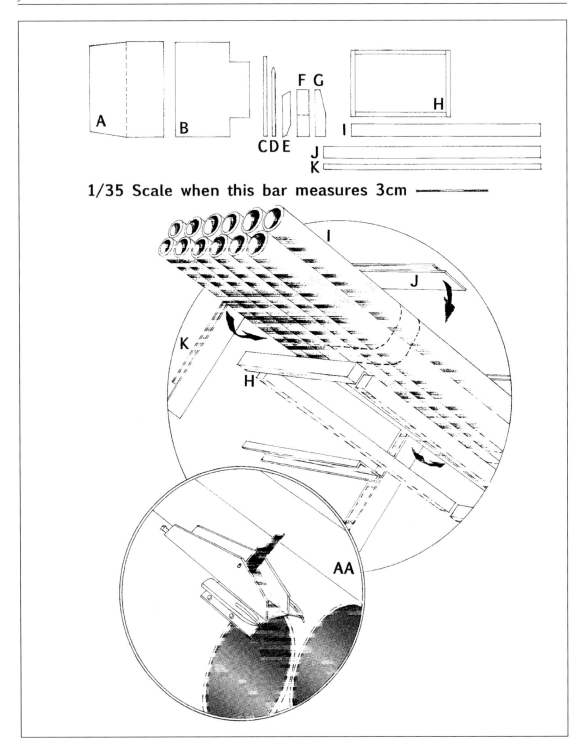

1/35 Scale when this bar measures 3cm

Fig. 4.26 *Templates and exploded diagrams.*

CHAPTER 5

T19 105mm Howitzer Gun Motor Carriage

Before the M7 105mm 'Priest' appeared in late 1942–3, the T19 half-track provided a very effective infantry support weapon, capable of traversing most types of terrain with comparative ease. The major advantage of this forward-firing combination over conventional towed artillery was ease and immediacy of use. The T19 mounting suffered from a tendency to be top-heavy. However, following initial fears of the heavy recoil being too much for the chassis and mounting, it acquitted itself very well under combat conditions. At times it was used in direct, close support of infantry – in much the same way as the German 'Marder' series of vehicles – and some were still in use at the war's end and beyond.

The Tamiya half-track kit is a 1970s gem. There are some compromises but it makes up into an excellent representation of the basic vehicle, with plenty of conversion potential. Watch out for ejector pin marks on exposed internal surfaces: stand by with the filler and fine emery paper, as they can be an eyesore. The after-market companies, particularly Verlinden, produce some excellent suspension/track upgrades in resin and, by the time storage is applied, it is possible to spend a fair chunk of money. The 105mm howitzer is the early 1980s Italeri offering. As with the half-track, there are a good many upgrades available, though the basic model is extremely sound and a testament to the Italian mould-cutter's art of old. There are US half-track kits available from DML and Trumpeter now, all eminently suitable for conversion.

This is one of those vehicles that was subject to minor detail differences. I have seen them with both the front bumper-mounted winch and, more commonly, the 'roller' unditching variant. This will inevitably dictate your choice of kit. I saw this sub-version in the Clint Eastwood film *Kelly's Heroes* years ago and thought back then that it was 'pretty cool'.

CONSTRUCTION

Referring to the Tamiya 81mm mortar-carrier kit instructions, build the vehicle in its entirety but leave out the whole of the fighting compartment interior and its detail. Even though it counts as stowage, replace the fuel can handles with ones from the Tamiya Allied Vehicles Accessories Set as they have three handles moulded separately, as opposed to the two-handled, inaccurate types moulded in the kit.

Retain kit part C28, the fighting compartment floor, and remove the petrol tanks at each side rear from part C27 (mortar crew floor). Cut out two off side floor template A (from 30 thou sheet) and cement in place against the fighting compartment walls (Fig. 5.1). Take care to trim and dry-fit until the edges are flush. The petrol tanks will both need 20 thou infill panels to their forward sides (Fig. 5.2), the exact size of which will depend on your dexterity with the piercing-saw. Once in place at the hull rear, they should be 'retained' with two 35mm 20 thou strips to each side.

Template D will fit in the body side 'kinks' where the front doors occur (Fig. 5.3), behind

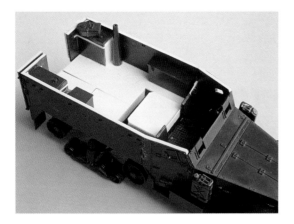

Fig. 5.1 *Relationship of gun-mounting base to ammunition stowage lockers.*

Fig. 5.2 *Forward fighting compartment bulkhead and side retainers.*

Fig. 5.3 *Front crew seat uprights are flush with the bulkhead.*

Fig. 5.4 *External stowage box and open rear door.*

Fig. 5.5 *Main armament underside with mountings in place.*

the front seats. It should be cut from 30 thou sheet and retained at each 'wall' end with small slivers of L-angle strip to suit the height.

The positioning of various boxes and the machine-gun pintle mounting for the .50-calibre Browning can be gauged from the photos and the plans/elevations supplied and Fig. 5.4. If the rear door is to be modelled in the open position, template B in 15 thou sheet should be placed between the rear body sides (Fig. 5.5), below the position of the opened door. Take care to trim the hinges so that the door will sit properly on the raised hinge portions on the body rear wall to the right.

Fig. 5.6 *Gun mountings in place.*

Template C, in its four portions, should then be placed in the positions shown in the drawings on the rear compartment floor (Fig. 5.6). Below them, the storage box walls separate the area into four distinct quadrants, with a lid for each one and with a forward 'wall' common to the front two. They should all be cut from 20 thou sheet and have hinges from 2mm plastic strip on the outer edges as shown.

Using the front windscreen drawing as a guide, remove the portion at the windshield's armoured top edge by first scoring with a craft knife, then removing with fine pliers. Trim and, if necessary, sand the resultant portion until clean and smooth. This will result in the gun being able to be depressed to its full extent once in place (Fig. 5.7).

Cut out the gun mounting platform from 20 thou sheet. Using template components E, F (×2), G (×2) and H (×2), construct the platform as shown in the exploded diagram, making sure that (after the glue has cured) the component is placed on the floor of the fighting compartment

Fig. 5.7 *Windscreen positioned after trimming.*

Fig. 5.8 *Main armament mounting's disposition.*

and pushed forward so that it sits flush with component D, the front bulkhead.

Circled portion L in the exploded diagram/template shows the main armament's lower mounting brackets (two off) made up from 20 thou, 4mm-wide strips. These locate on the bottom portion of the gun's main mounting cross member (Fig. 5.8). The inner windshield should be omitted, as no glazing was desirable in

the vicinity of the 105mm howitzer's muzzle blast. Often, the headlights were removed and/or replaced with later-pattern blast-proof items.

The top edge of each of the armoured walls should have 2mm, 10 thou strip glued in place as shown in the exploded view.

The howitzer can be taken from one of two currently available Italeri kits, either the weapon on its field carriage or, as in my case, from their excellent M7 Priest howitzer motor carriage. The latter also provides an excellent source of spare parts including stowage, a machine gun, jerrycans and, best of all, ammunition (Fig. 5.9).

As in Fig. 5.8, the mounting brackets from circled portion L in the exploded diagram should be cemented in place on the howitzer's main mounting cross-member. With a dry run, check that they remain 'inboard' of the edges of component E, the gun mounting's top plate.

I found it easier to paint the gun and the half-track as separate sub-assemblies (Figs 5.10 and 5.11). You may like to consider this, as the gun has some quite delicate components such as the sighting equipment and, when taken as a whole,

Fig. 5.9 *First paint coat in place.*

Fig. 5.10 *Stowage from various sources.*

Fig. 5.11 *Rear door can be modelled open or closed.*

the two together can be quite cumbersome to handle during painting.

Stowage items are really down to individual taste and reference shots. As a quick guide, though, try to imagine that you are stowing your equipment: where would you put it for safety, ease of access and sheer practicality? I used Dragon, Tamiya and Italeri accessories but VLS, Accurate Armour and many other companies produce a wide variety of beautifully moulded plastic and resin accessories.

Remember that backpacks and similar can be stored on a flat surface or, indeed, hung on various cleats and brackets around the vehicle. Their straps, often omitted by manufacturers, can be made from plastic, paper, or even zinc strip (from oil paint tubes) quite easily. Bear in mind that they all have their own unique 'working' methods and all behave slightly differently during manufacture of components.

PAINTING

I sprayed the model overall using Humbrol matt green 30. A base coat was applied, then two further light 'dust coats' with a three-hour gap in between (Figs 5.12 and 5.13). A light dusting with a thinned pale stone colour/white was sparingly applied after the whole had been 'shadowed' in the panel recesses with thinned matt black. Scratches and scuffs were plentiful on these vehicles, especially when they were used in the harsh scrubland around Kasserine Pass and, later on, in Italy. I applied many: older ones in black and rust, with the more recent ones left in plain metal shades. A good deal of dry brushing then occurred with a pale sand/stone mix, and graphite for surface scuffs to the interior floors.

All in all this is a good intermediate conversion with some interesting sand/dark green/black camouflage options to ring the changes in what, if one is not careful, rapidly becomes a khaki drab collection of US vehicles!

Fig. 5.12 *Rear view with weathering.*

Fig. 5.13 *Front three-quarter view with weathering.*

Fig. 5.14 *Wintering in Italy.*

Fig. 5.15 *Elevation with side/windscreens collapsed.*

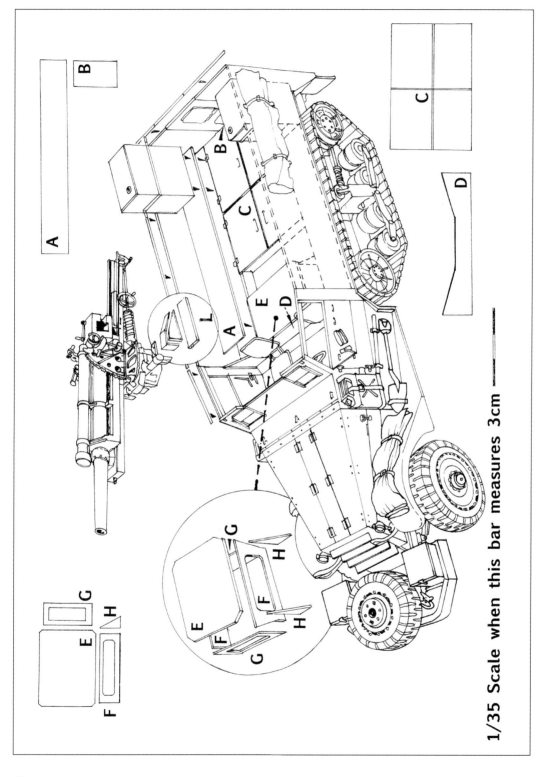

1/35 Scale when this bar measures 3cm

Fig. 5.16 *Exploded view with templates.*

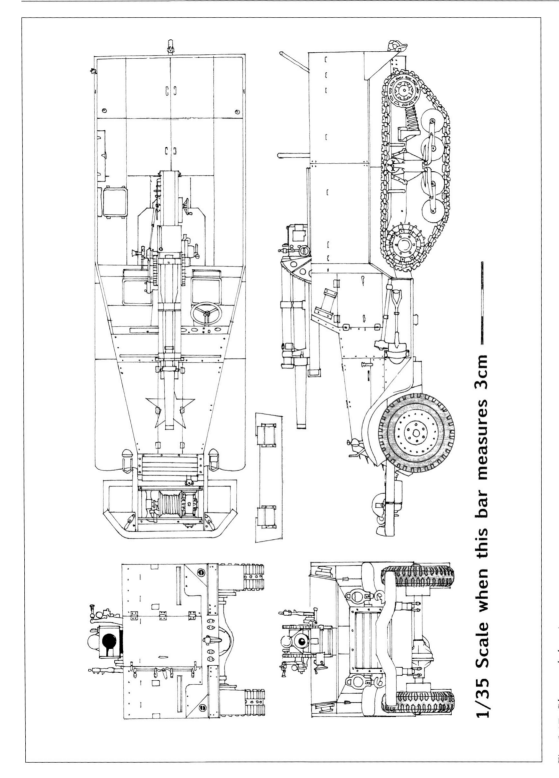

1/35 Scale when this bar measures 3cm ▬▬

Fig. 5.17 *Plans and elevations.*

Fig. 5.18 *Dashboard, front roller and winch options.*

Fig. 5.19 *Right side rear – note track running on top roller.*

Fig. 5.20 *Left side front – complete.*

CHAPTER 6

Panther *Raketenwerfer* (Skoda)

In the opening stages of Operation *Barbarossa*, Hitler's lightning-fast advances using blitzkrieg techniques shocked, but did not stun the Soviet war machine, which soon recovered to stem and then reverse the German advance. The Soviets' *Katyusha* rocket systems were a very effective way to use otherwise useless, inaccurately machined shells to help stem the German advances, particularly around Stalingrad and Moscow.

The German *Nebelwerfer* rocket system is well documented. However, before the war's end, Skoda in German-occupied Czechoslovakia produced drawings for this, the Panther *Raketenwerfer*, combining 105mm rockets in calibre-uncritical frame launchers with what would have been exceptional mobility from the Panther tank chassis. Although only ever a 'paper Panzer', it is not difficult to imagine this extraordinarily

Fig. 6.1 Raketenwerfer *in action*.

modern-looking machine's battlefield debut. By late 1944, though, there were precious few Panther chassis available or, indeed, any other vehicle types. It is testament to the design that many of the multi-launch rocket systems seen on battlefields today use precisely this design solution.

This vehicle was not, to my knowledge and after extensive research, 'alive' in anything but the designer's mind or the sheaves of paper on Skoda's drawing boards. It is not difficult to imagine, though, just how effective it would have been in combat.

When firing with the launch rails in different attitudes, problems may have been encountered with blast and rocket exhaust entering the rails and engine air-intakes on the rear decking. You may want to make some further assumptions than those of mine, and build blast shields/baffles to protect these components.

KIT AND SCALE CHOICE

The conversion is built on Italeris' 1/72 scale Panther, as the detail is excellent. You could, of course, cannibalize several other kits if you wanted all-steel road wheels, as per the elevations provided. It is worth bearing in mind, though, that these vehicles would have been far

more likely to be built around older chassis, which would have been returned to homeland factories from the front line for rebuilding with the rocket system.

The so-called 'braille-scale' of 1/72 originally came about in the 1960s to complement Airfix Models' series of military vehicle kits in their usage with HO/OO model railways, and may seem like a strange place to start with a 'paper panzer'. The smaller scales have, however, seen a great resurgence in popularity in recent years, as you can have a very large and diverse model collection in a relatively small space. They are ideal for war-gaming and the recent release of many new items by Dragon and others has provided for a very well detailed selection at very reasonable prices.

CONSTRUCTION

For the purposes shown here, I used Italeri's Panther Ausf A for the hull/running gear. The rocket cradle central-pivot mechanism was taken from the now very old but excellent value 1/72 scale German '88mm gun and tractor' kit from Airfix, which I believe dates from the 1960s!

Take the lower hull and complete as per the kit instructions. However, please note that from this point onward the changes and additions to the

Fig. 6.2 *The hull top infill plate in position.*

Fig. 6.3 *Lower hull rear infill portions.*

sponson/chassis areas will vary, depending on whose kit you choose.

I first cut out two pieces from 30 thou sheet to 'infill' the rear third of the chassis upper side armour plates (Fig. 6.2). You should fill and sand these to a common surface: this is much better than re-making the side-chassis armour, and the results are virtually invisible when complete.

The upper hull then requires the turret ring, aperture and surrounding armour to be cut out and replaced by a 20 thou plastic panel (Fig. 6.3) measuring 30 × 35mm wide. The correct placing of this panel requires it to butt up to the leading edge of the forward engine vents.

Turn the upper hull assembly on its back and add the two sponson infill panels (Fig. 6.4), again

Fig. 6.4 *Sponson bottom plates and hull top infill supports.*

Fig. 6.5 *Hull top kit detail parts added.*

from 20 thou strip or sheet. They each should measure 10 × 78mm in length and will marry to the inner face of the sloped rear engine panel.

Once you have mated the top and bottom hulls (Fig. 6.5), refer to the scale drawings for the exact position of the 88mm gun mounting pedestal, which should be carefully cut out from the cruciform base in the Airfix kit and cemented in place on the new hull top panel.

Assemble the gun cradle and its side brackets (Fig. 6.6), removing the kit's two recoil recuperator damper tubes from the bottom cradle and replace with two 30 × 2.5mm tubes in the positions shown. This is a good time to grab your references and add any super-detailing you might see fit.

Fig. 6.6 *Hull carrying gun cradle. Side brackets with mounting attached.*

Fig. 6.7 *Templates J, ready for assembly.*

Fig. 6.8 *Recuperator tubes and rocket frames in place.*

With careful attention to the template sheet, manufacture eight off component J from angled and straight 'evergreen' strip, taking care to check that they are 'square' at each turn (Fig. 6.7). Join them in two banks, as shown in the exploded view and Fig. 6.8, using twelve off 13mm width spacing bars (20 thou × 1.5mm) and template piece K for the vertical side bars (six off).

Refer again to the elevations to place four off template L diagonally in position, on the left or outer side of the rocket launcher frame assembly (Fig. 6.9). Template M is then added to brace the inner side of the upper of the two launch rail banks, as shown in the exploded view.

Study the rear launch rail photograph. Between it and the exploded view, it will become apparent how the 1mm rod should be cut and assembled to effect the pivot linkage system and its sychronization with the two recuperator dampers below (Fig. 6.10).

The cabin on the opposite side of the gun brackets should likewise be assembled from template components A to I, with reference to the accompanying diagram and Figs 6.11 and 6.12. Components A and B (two off each) make up the cabin's bottom. The strengthening rail (C and D)

Fig. 6.9 *Rocket frame rear three-quarter view.*

Fig. 6.10 *Fire control box rear door – note position of elevation linkage to rear of recuperator tubes.*

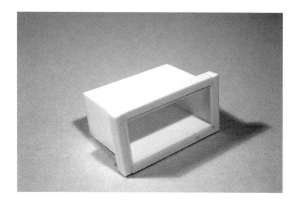

Fig. 6.11 *Templates A, B, C and D assembled.*

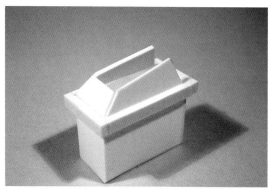

Fig. 6.12 *E and F templates in place.*

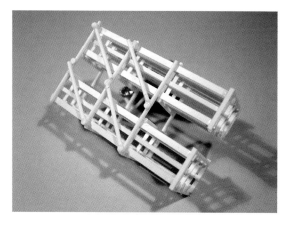

Fig. 6.13 *Template K (×4) and their pivoting bolts between.*

Fig. 6.14 *Elevation linkage and fire control box mounting – note position of template M.*

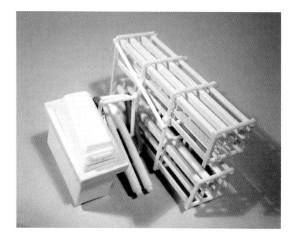

Fig. 6.15 *Fire control box in place.*

Fig. 6.16 *Preferred launch position to ensure that no damage occurs to the rear engine decking.*

should be built from 2.5 × 2mm plastic strip. When cutting these pieces, take care to cut off the ends absolutely square, ensuring that as little filler as possible is used.

The cabin top should be built using components E to I, cut from 20 thou sheet and a vision slit, 6 × 2mm, placed on its front panel. Sand and finish the whole, checking for squareness throughout construction.

At this point, add all of the tools, jacks and so on to the upper hull (Fig. 6.16) and (if you prefer) before painting, add the nicely detailed link-and-length track, making sure to build in the correct amount of 'track-sag'.

I have made a few assumptions during the construction of this model, which I think is fair, bearing in mind that it never actually existed. I, therefore, think that 'blast-shields' and an ammunition-carrying vehicle, possibly on the same type of chassis, would be an excellent diorama subject: one that will really give your imagination free rein!

PAINTING

I sprayed the whole vehicle with two light coats of Tamiya pale sand. Once dry, some 'shadowing' with a mid-grey/thinners mix, followed by a fine 'filter' coat of mid-stone gave a perfect base for the 'giraffe' camouflage scheme seen in the later stages of the war on the Russian front. Any of the late-war camouflages, 'splinter', three-colour, 'ambush' or even – if the conjecture that this old paint was reintroduced as stocks of others ran low late in the war is correct – 'Panzer grey' would suit this vehicle well.

The beauty of this 'rail' multi-launch rocket system would have been its adaptability, especially if the rails had been built on a 'slotted-bar' basis, allowing for different calibres and configurations of projectiles to be launched after wing-nuts had been adjusted. Captured *Katyusha* rockets would have been especially suitable for this purpose.

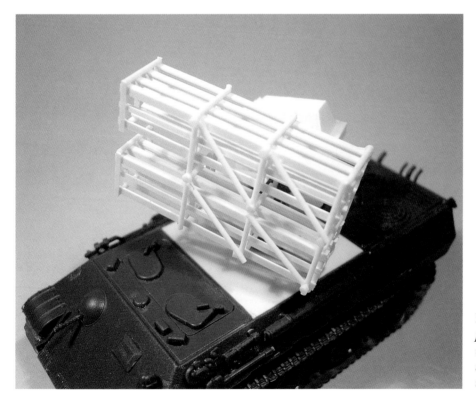

Fig. 6.17 *Note position of cross-wise strengtheners to top of rocket rails.*

Fig. 6.18 *Tracks of link and length type require great care during assembly.*

Fig. 6.19 *Two coats of base colour.*

Fig. 6.20 *Don't forget the vision slit to fire-control box front.*

Fig. 6.21 *Shadow coating carefully applied where necessary.*

Fig. 6.22 *The finished article, front right.*

Fig. 6.23 *Rear left three-quarter view.*

Fig. 6.24 *Panther rear, tools and exhaust details.*

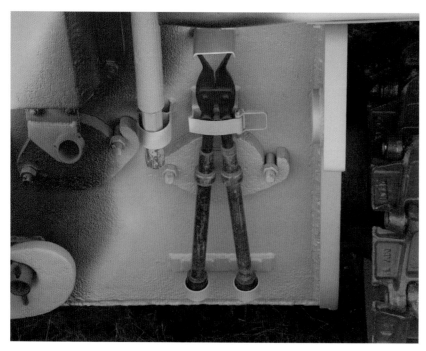

Fig. 6.25 *Panther wire cutters detail.*

Fig. 6.26 *Panther engine decking.*

Fig. 6.27 *Panther drive sprocket detail.*

Fig. 6.28 *Panther air intake cover detail.*

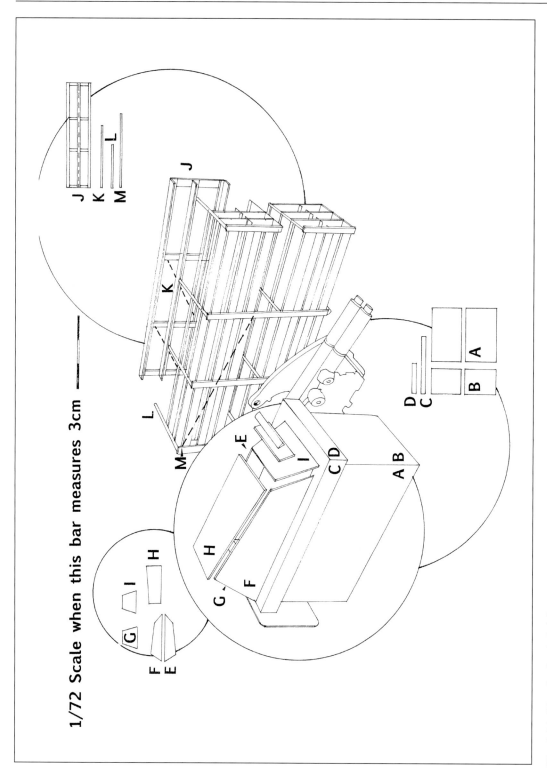

1/72 Scale when this bar measures 3cm

Fig. 6.29 *Template/exploded diagram.*

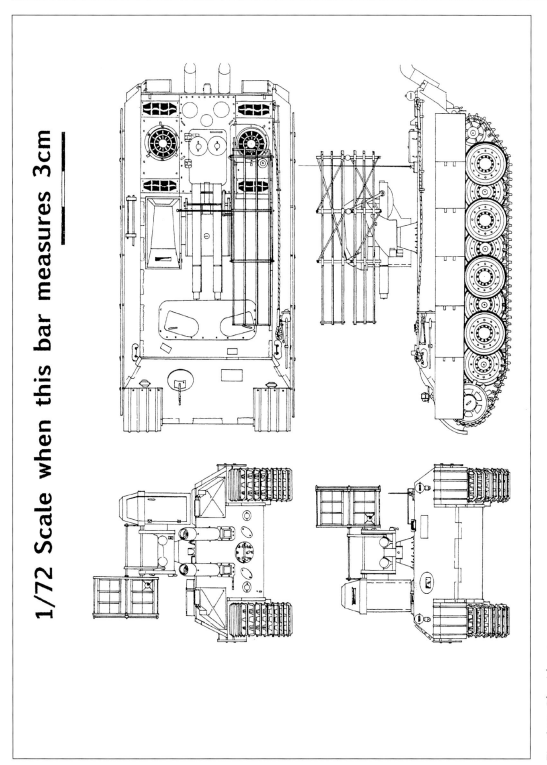

1/72 Scale when this bar measures 3cm

Fig. 6.30 *Plans/elevations.*

CHAPTER 7

KV3 *Obiekt* 220

Unfortunately for the Soviet military, the KV3 *Obiekt* 220 prototype remained exactly that – a one-off. In late 1940, whilst the German Panther and Tiger were still pipe dreams, Russian designers (whilst working on the revolutionary T34 design) managed to produce this startling heavy tank with an 85mm F-30 main armament and the capacity to up-gun to 122mm. Its ammunition load of ninety-one 85mm rounds and 4,032 rounds for its three Degtyarev machine guns meant that a speed of only 33km/h (20mph)

would have been achievable. This was not a large problem, however, when one considers its excellent use of ballistic armour plate, soon to become legendary in battle on the KV1 and 2. The Klimenti Voroshilov (KV) series was well known for its ability to absorb punishment. KV1s were often found with upward of fifty hits from various calibres of ammunition up to 75mm, yet still fully operational.

The Trumpeter kits (you will need two) are of the new and quite excellent KV2 tank model.

Fig. 7.1 *Hypothetical 'combat' shot.*

The standard of moulding is remarkable, with excellent surface detail and ejector pin marks in very sensible places. There is a choice of either styrene link-and-length tracks, or rubberized PVC versions. Both have excellent surface detail and take very little work to look absolutely realistic. Worthy of note, also, is the quality of the plastic. Being perfectly rigid, and accepting all of the normal glues excellently, it is also very easy to cut and carve accurately.

CONSTRUCTION

The Trumpeter kit of the KV2 is more than a little bit special, the construction of the main hull being a case in point. The hull lower sides are individual and affix to the sides of a central 'bath' casting in what turns out for us to be a happy accident: when the components are altered and fixed together, their juxtapositions result in a very strong structure.

The KV3 had one extra road wheel on each side. To achieve this, referring to the photographs and plan drawings, firstly cut the kit's chassis sides vertically, using a set square or an engineer's try-square, immediately to the rear of the third swinging-arm hole and then again, 11mm forward of the third-from-rear rebound rubber mounting. Separate the two components, discarding the centre third. From the second kit's chassis sides, cut out the centre portion – as you will note in the photograph – with two swinging arm pivot holes in the centre (Fig. 7.2). This centre portion will then measure 49mm in length. Refer to the elevations before any cuts are made, and double-check dimensions before the final chopping occurs. Glue the resultant portions together and lie them flat to dry.

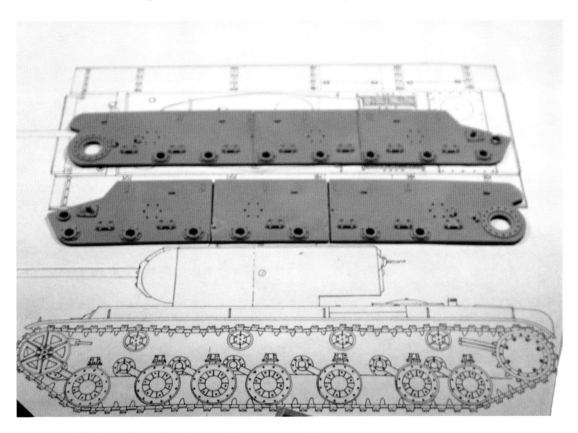

Fig. 7.2 *Hull sides – refer to plan drawings for exact cut positions.*

Fig. 7.3 *Allow the sub-assemblies to dry thoroughly before final fixing of hull parts.*

Fig. 7.4 *Lower hull infill piece in place. Sand joints, and fill until level.*

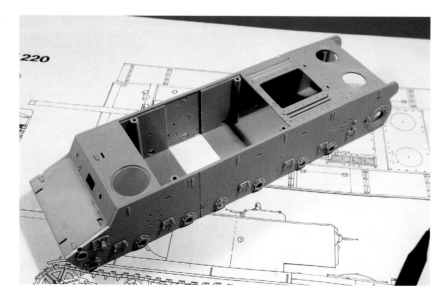

Fig. 7.5 *Upper hull cutting points for removal of turret ring section.*

Meanwhile, cut the central bath portion – preferably, with a good deal of care, using a piercing saw or jigsaw, as shown in Fig. 7.3. The cut should be exactly halfway between the forward four vertical location tubes on the bath's inner faces. Then glue the outer sides to the inner bath structure (Figs 7.4 and 7.5), which will have its resultant underside gap filled with the smaller of the two unlabelled sheets from the template drawing: this fills the 23 × 49mm gap exactly.

Turning to the hull top, Fig. 7.6 shows the exact position of the second unlabelled hull make-up piece from the drawing, between the front glacis plate upper and the leading edge of the rear engine decking. After chopping the upper hull amidships, dry-run these portions in place, testing the new piece in its location (cut from 30 thou sheet), noting the exact places where the kit portions need to be cut to accommodate the new turret ring section. Glue all the parts together, and leave them to dry. This will result in a structure with great integrity and strength.

The track-top fenders must, likewise, be chopped and extended (Figs 7.7 and 7.8). On each side, chop the fenders and remove the centre section from behind the second cantilever support from the front, and repeat the process once more after the second cantilever support

Fig. 7.6 *New turret ring section in place.*

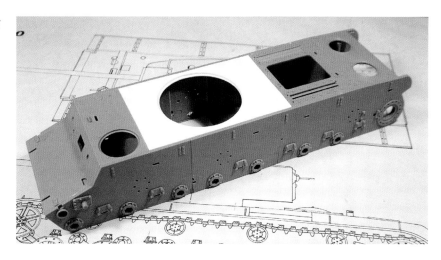

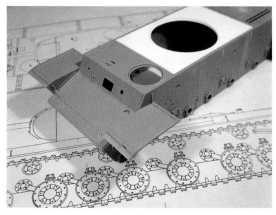

Fig. 7.7 *Front of track-guards in place, with central bracket clips removed.*

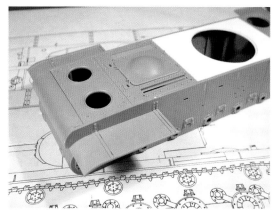

Fig. 7.8 *Rear track-guard portions in situ, awaiting centre section.*

from the rear. Trim off the upright brackets for the centremost cantilever struts and, when re-finished, replace it with suitable plastic strip. The extra cantilever bracing piece on each side can be taken from the second donor kit, the positions of which can be ascertained from the plans and relevant photographs. The fender make-up strips measure 125 × 19.5mm each and must be inserted only after the front and rear portions are in place. Some trimming may be necessary to achieve an exact fit.

The shell deflector, forward of the turret ring, is made from two 2.5 × 28mm strips, cemented in place with its apex central, each strip making an angle of 26 degrees to the presumed horizontal when viewed from the front of the vehicle.

Now the addition of all the kit parts can begin. Noting positions on the side elevation, fix on all swinging arms, wheels, rebound brackets, return rollers and their mountings, front idlers and, finally, the rear drive sprocket assemblies, being careful to fix the mud-deflector brackets carefully after them to prevent any kind of distortion of those parts.

Three storage bins are required in the positions shown, and two dual-length track links were added to complete the upper hull stowage. Note that, for the engine rear armour and the bow armour/glacis plate, the kit instructions should be followed. Finally, on the upper hull, I filled in the turret ring with a sandwich of three 30 thou, 44mm diameter discs, cut carefully with the circle cutter before snapping out of the plastic sheet. These fit into the kit's turret ring infill piece, used as a lower turret ring on the underside of the turret.

THE TURRET

Using the template drawing, carefully cut out the turret components A, B, C and D, plus two off part E. Assemble A, B and C as per the accompanying exploded diagram, with C vertical between the other two, forming a stepped turret base (Figs 7.9 and 7.10). Then add the turret sides, E, making sure of their squareness to the turret base. The resultant gaps, front and rear

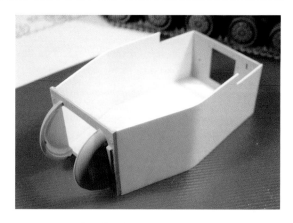

Fig. 7.9 *Underside of turret assembly before addition of turret bottom/ring components.*

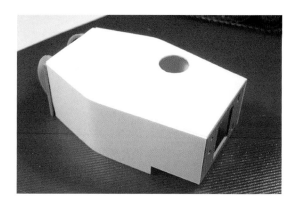

Fig. 7.10 *Turret front and rear plates are cut from relevant kit components.*

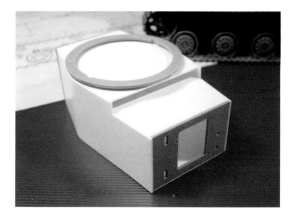

Fig. 7.11 *Turret ring added, with reference to plan drawings.*

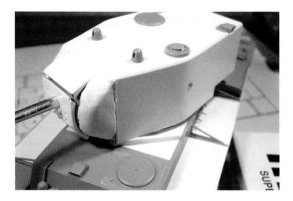

Fig. 7.12 *Filler added to mantlet edge-trims.*

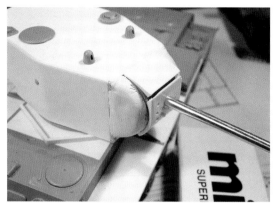

Fig. 7.13 *Sub-turret shell deflector in place.*

Fig. 7.14 *Add mantlet edge-trims and extra outer portion to outer pivot mechanism housing.*

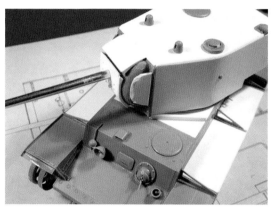

Fig. 7.15 *Mantlet edge-trims before filler is added.*

between the turret sides, will accommodate the turret front and rear plates from the donor kit (Fig. 7.11), after they have been trimmed along their sides and bottom edges; refer to the photographs for exact proportions. Add the rear turret door and accompanying fitments but, on the turret front, apply Milliput as per Figs 7.12 and 7.13 to achieve the significant 'cheek' bulges to the sides of the gun-mantlet's pivot mounting. The Milliput should be of a 'rough-cast' appearance, so do not go overboard with the wet and dry paper.

The front protrusion of the kit's gun mantlet then needs to be reduced in size (by saw or grinder) until it is flush with the curve of the mantlet. Build up the new mantlet front and

hinged top protection plate with 30 thou sheet (Figs 7.14 and 7.15), whilst referring to the elevations and exploded diagram.

The turret top, D, needs the stereoscopic ranging episcopes added from the kit in the positions shown on the drawings (Fig. 7.16); likewise with the circular gunner's hatch and periscopes shown on the turret's left and right rear (Fig. 7.17). The air vent forward of the commander's cupola was taken directly from the donor kit. The commander's cupola was manufactured from plastic tube, strip and sheet in the manner shown in Fig. 7.18. Judicious trimming and sanding of all components is required throughout assembly. Finally, once the turret is assembled,

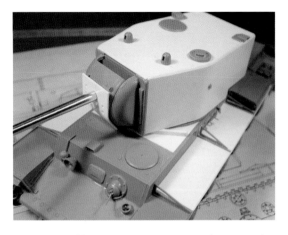

Fig. 7.16 *Add turret top components and gun mantlet.*

Fig. 7.17 *Track-guard centre portions with edge trimming and mantlet top added.*

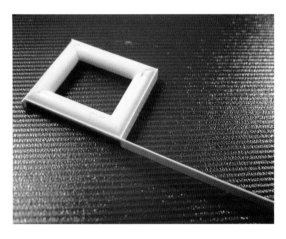

Fig. 7.18 *Commander's cupola construction.*

a 45-degree chamfer should be added to the top edge of each facet of the turret side/top. This can be 'pared' by drawing the blade away from you at a 45-degree angle, or with fine emery paper around a small wooden block (or similar), until the chamfer measures 2mm in depth.

In the reference drawings and photographs I have managed to amass, there are two different types of commander's cupola. I have fixed the type shown on the Russian plans, as the pictures of the actual tank available on the web are quite clear and will be relatively easy for you to find and replicate accurately.

The main armament I used (Fig. 7.19) is an aluminium-turned 85mm weapon (as used on

Fig. 7.19 *Commander's cupola MG in position.*

the T34/85). However, it was intended that the tank would be able to be up-gunned in service to use the 122mm weapon that became available later. By the look of the turret, it would have been able to be used with the 152mm gun before the war's end.

I do not doubt that if these tanks had been available in sufficient quantities in 1941, Operation *Barbarossa* – Hitler's invasion of Russia – could have been a huge flash in the pan!

PAINTING

The whole vehicle was sprayed in Humbrol matt light olive in two coats (Figs 7.20–7.23), twenty-four hours apart. Shadows and general shading were then added with the airbrush in matt dark olive thinned 50–50 with white spirit (Fig. 7.24) and applied with two hours between each of the three applications. On top of that, two coats of thinned pale sand (in patches to replicate road dust) were applied, and then a final dry-brush

Fig. 7.20 *Disposition of stowage bins.*

Fig. 7.21 *Lower hull rear details. Note tow-shackles hanging vertically.*

Fig. 7.22 *Rear turret MG in place.*

Fig. 7.23 *Turret top details. Note, with kit components, check the exact positions on plan drawings.*

Fig. 7.24 *'Shadow' coat applied before weathering is applied.*

Fig. 7.25 *KV3 with tank riders.*

application of a white/sand 50–50 mix in the places most likely to suffer whilst on campaign. Rust smears in oil pastel and scratches with a fine 000 paintbrush finish the tank, except for the tracks (Fig. 7.25).

EXTENDING THE TRACKS

As the extra road wheel each side dictates major surgery to the hull sides, so the tracks need to be lengthened to suit. The vinyl tracks will require an extra portion, ten links in length, from those in the second kit. The plastic link-and-length tracks will require eleven or twelve extra links each side if track-sag is to be replicated accurately. However, when making this decision you should bear in mind that unfortunately – and according to the best sources – this tank did not see combat. Then again, a 'what-if' diorama featuring it with a knocked-out Tiger tank would make an interesting talking point!

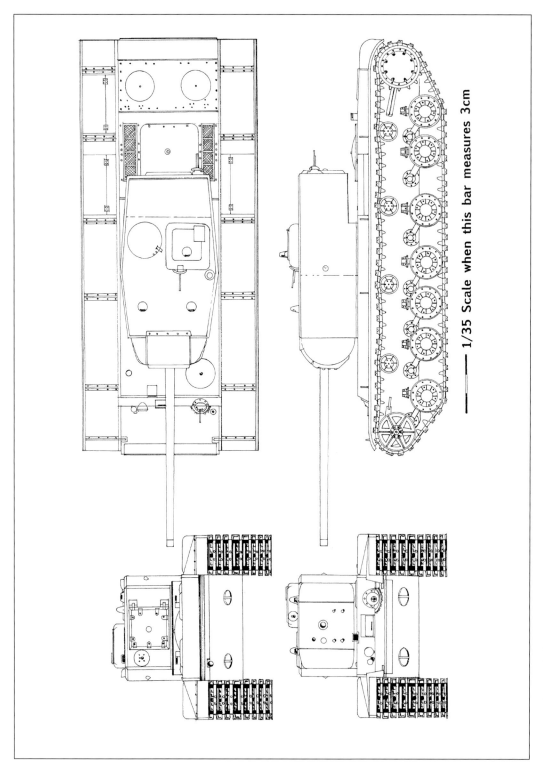

Fig. 7.26 *Plans and elevations.*

1/35 Scale when this bar measures 3cm

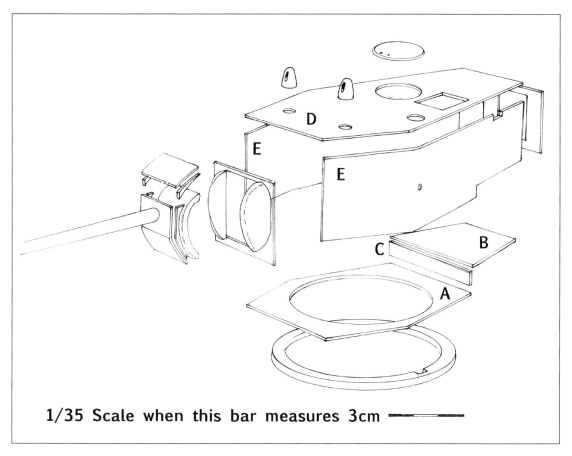

1/35 Scale when this bar measures 3cm ▬▬▬

Fig. 7.27 *Exploded diagram – turret.*

Fig. 7.28 *KV3* Obiekt *220, alternative turret type.*

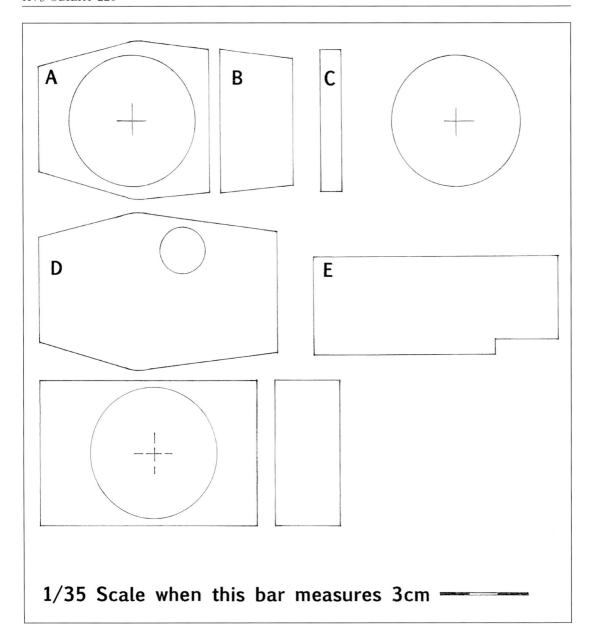

Fig. 7.29 *Turret template.*

CHAPTER 8

M31 Lee ARVII

Throughout the relatively short history of armoured warfare there has always been a desperate need for battlefield recovery vehicles, however expedient. The M31, although extemporized on an M3 Lee chassis, provided an excellent solution to the problem. It often recovered and towed Shermans and heavy self-propelled artillery with its 27-ton capacity winch, mounted in the main compartment. Its power was transmitted, via a purpose-built boom with twin telescopic supports, through a hawser that was, at a pinch, capable of dragging around 40 tons.

Fig. 8.1 *Ardennes, 1944, or is it?*

The Tamiya kit on which this conversion is based is now over thirty years old. It is, however, (at this scale) out on its own in terms of availability and extraordinary value. There are some dimensional problems and 1970s construction compromises, most notable of which is the lack of armour to the undersides of the sponsons. Even with some compromises this is still an excellent basis for conversion, and extremely cost effective. An Academy kit is now available, and has had more than its share of rave reviews – tough choice!

Reference and research is, as always, a pre-requisite for a conversion on this scale. There are a good many photographs available in various publications, often showing detail differences from vehicle to vehicle. The most notable difference that I have seen was the addition of a .50-calibre machine gun and skate-rail to the turret top; I presume that it came from the M8 Greyhound armoured car. If my reference picture had been clearer, I would have included it here – happy hunting!

This build is fairly advanced but, if taken carefully, one step at a time, can be completed by a comparative novice. Bear in mind that, however many conversions we undertake, our model-making apprenticeships tend to last a lifetime! There is always a new technique to be learned or, indeed, invented.

Constant cross-reference will be needed throughout the build. Once the templates have been cut, however, all of the necessary dimensions and build sequences can be gleaned from the drawings, in-build shots and exploded views. Super detailing of the interior will demand a little extra research on your part, but is achievable. The French tank museum at Saumur still retains an original vehicle.

STARTING CONSTRUCTION

First, assemble the lower hull and running gear as per the instructions in the Tamiya kit. I added the solid, six-spoke wheels from the excellent Dragon Red Army M4 Sherman (Fig. 8.2) to correspond with reference shots in my possession. I

Fig. 8.2 *New Sherman road and return wheels with rear sponson infill detail.*

Fig. 8.3 *Front sponson joint – trim to fit.*

Fig. 8.4 *Left side front sponson infill showing edge detail.*

must assume that these were used in preference to the open-spoke types on the original for their increased weight, as an aid to traction and for heavy lifts.

When complete, join the lower hull to the assembled panels of the upper hull/glacis plate and rear engine decking. The holes below the sponsons along each side of the hull should be filled (Fig. 8.3) using two off from template M (from 30 thou sheet). Carefully trim and pare the outer edges with a scalpel or similar, until they are flush with the body sides (Fig. 8.4).

Referring to the exploded drawing/template, cut components E and F from 30 thou plastic strip/sheet and glue them at 90 degrees to one another, as per Fig. 8.5, on the rear edge of the engine decking. Add the roller/retaining brackets from 40 thou strip, trimmed to shape, and use return rollers from any spare Sherman suspension components that you may have to hand. If none is available, a suitable sprue can be used quite successfully if the relevant holes are drilled in each cut end.

Referring again to the relevant reference, the new rear engine-deck storage lockers can be assembled *in situ* using templates A, B, C and D as a starting point (from 30 thou sheet). Part B in its entirety will make the outer panel of the right side storage locker (Fig. 8.6). The right-hand portion will be the outer panel of the left-hand one. Two of template D will make their rear panels and two of part C will be their forward infills, whilst the right-hand portion of part A and the whole of A will be the right and left locker's inboard infill panels. The remaining panels/ends can then be easily measured and cut out, before adding them – along with the locker lids (Fig. 8.7), from 15mm-wide 20 thou strip – with hinges/hasps and locks to suit. This will all be much clearer after careful study of the relevant in-build shots.

The hole in the main armament hull sponson should be infilled using two off 23 × 9mm pieces of 20 thou sheets (Fig. 8.8). These, along with the three hinges, form the new hull door, hinged along its inboard edge. The 'false' gun barrel seen in the photos is the kit part B31, made to resemble the imitation gun of the original.

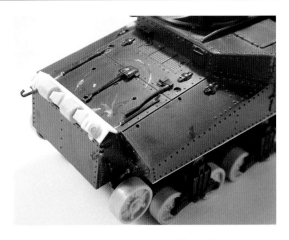

Fig. 8.5 *Templates E and F assembled. The return rollers are still minus central bolts.*

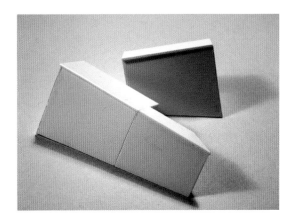

Fig. 8.6 *Rear hull stowage boxes complete, minus hinges.*

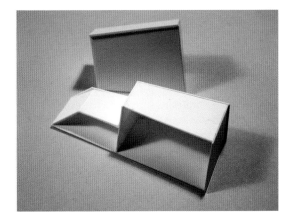

Fig. 8.7 *Rear hull stowage boxes – underside.*

Fig. 8.8 *New front door and false gun detail.*

Fig. 8.9 *Extra stowage boxes – front.*

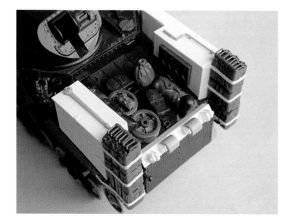

Fig. 8.10 *Rear hull stowage.*

Fig. 8.11 *Final hull assembly with crew stowage in place.*

The three extra storage boxes on the hull front (Fig. 8.9) have lids measuring 20 × 15mm (glacis plate), 12 × 15mm (gun sponson top) and 16 × 12mm for the one immediately in front of the turret. All of these have hinges and hasps/locks added, with reference to the pictures/plans. The drive sprocket inboard bulged castings (kit parts B38 and B39) have tiny U-shaped brackets whilst B20 (the front rounded bow-plate) has a simple bracket construction to carry the forward towing hook as shown in the in-build shots.

Then, storage – and plenty of it. The bracketed fuel cans on the hull rear (Figs 8.10 and 8.11) correspond with a picture of a D-Day vehicle in American usage. The retaining straps are made from 2.5 × 46mm 10 thou plastic strip, wrapped around once the cans are glued in place. Affix all of the necessary kit parts, such as hatches, handles, brackets and vision ports.

THE TURRET AND BOOM ASSEMBLY

The plans show the turret traversed forward, which was sometimes preferred for 'sticky' pulls out of sucking mud or quicksand, using the reverse or 'crawler' gear. My vehicle has the turret traversed rearward (*see* Fig. 8.1) for a straight vehicle tow – the choice is yours. (Note that in the plans/elevations, the turret is traversed

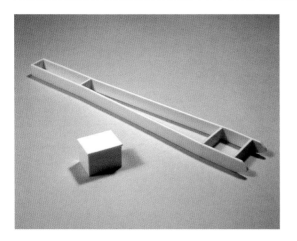

Fig. 8.12 *Boom lattice assembly.*

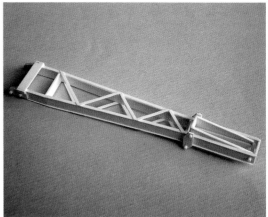

Fig. 8.13 *'U'-section girder detail.*

Fig. 8.14 *Note position of front towing hook below front bow winch plate.*

Fig. 8.15 *Completed boom assembly.*

forward.) When you have constructed kit parts A28, A29 and the gun shield, adding the 37mm gun barrel as a dummy to the turret rear, the boom construction beckons. The split commander's hatch is from the Tamiya 'early production' M4 but would be simple to produce from an 18mm-diameter 30 thou disc of sheet plastic, with plastic strip/rod detailing.

Referring to the turret/boom exploded diagram, cut two off templates G, H and I, respectively, in 30 thou sections. As seen in the in-build photograph, they bend slightly at the points indicated by dotted lines on template G.

H forms the two rearmost spacers, whilst I (×2) the foremost.

The top and bottom edges of the basic boom have 2mm plastic strip added to make parts G into U-section girders (Figs 8.12 and 8.13). Carry on with the 2mm strip as lattice bracing to the top and bottom, referring to the scale plans for exact disposition. At G's rounded pivot end, cut two similar-shaped, 14mm-long brackets, each with two large bolt heads. The bracing piece below these also carries a large, 3mm-thick counterweight, as seen in the finished build shots.

The winch main bracket is built up using templates J, K and L (from 30 thou sheet), plus 6mm-wide 20 thou strip for the infill portions to the assembly. This is then placed above the pivot point at the boom's base. The opposite end receives the forward winch cable bracket and side supports; dimensions for these can be measured directly from the scale drawings. Two pivoting brackets are then added to the turret gun port, and the whole boom assembly glued in place.

Two telescopic struts made from plastic rod and brass tubing, cut to length, support the boom. The lengths of these will vary by 3mm one to the other, as the geometry is not symmetrical (the turret being offset to the left-hand side of the vehicle). The hawsers and bracing wires were added from fine piano wire, being dulled in the process.

The tracks were from the Dragon Red Army M4 Sherman. This particular type of track, or indeed the 'Chevron' type, would provide a great deal more traction than the plain rubber block ones on soft ground or sand. The duck-bill extender type would also be an interesting departure, being available in the Tamiya late-production Sherman, or from several of the after-market manufacturers.

PAINTING

Paint was two coats of Humbrol matt green 30, carefully applied via aerosol over a period of twenty-four hours (Figs 8.16–8.19). The new-formula Humbrol enamels dry matt with a very slight sheen. As can be seen from many wartime photographs and preserved vehicles today, this gives a very realistic final representation; however, this is only if the vehicle is virtually factory-fresh.

Dry-brushing, application of sand and dust 'filter' coats with the airbrush resulted in a very well-worn vehicle, somewhere in the Low Countries in late 1944 (Figs 8.20 and 8.21). By this time, the large white star was out of favour with the allies as it made for a convenient aiming point for German anti-tank gunners. In spite of this, such a large vehicle operating in forward areas was often thus marked in order to reduce the instances of destruction from friendly fire, in the likely event that it was spotted by a 'Rhubarb' low-level Thunderbolt or Typhoon strike.

Fig. 8.16 *First two paint coats complete.*

Fig. 8.17 *New tool positions on lockers and hull side.*

Fig. 8.18 *First two coats for all the tank's nooks and crannies.*

Fig. 8.19 *Colours after first 'shadowing' paint coat.*

Fig. 8.20 *Rear left three-quarter view.*

Fig. 8.21 *Front right – note scratching to hull painted with a 000, olive drab-laden brush.*

M31 GENERAL LEE ARV WITH ASSAULT BRIDGE

During the latter part of 1943, the Allied assault on mainland Italy faltered momentarily as British, Commonwealth and American troops discovered just how hard was the so-called 'soft' underbelly of Europe that they had chosen to invade. After Rome had fallen, the German forces under Kesselring headed north, where the rough terrain, fast-flowing rivers and torturous ravines made any but the most cautious of advances positively suicidal.

German engineers had become, by this time, extraordinarily well practised in bridge destruction in order to slow the Allied advance. Lessons learned in Italy by the Allies eventually gave rise to the Churchill AVRE bridge-laying tanks created by Major General Percy Hobart's 'Funnies' team, which were used in the D-Day landings in Normandy. The first such specialized vehicle, though, was extemporized on the Lee chassis in Italy in 1943, and was to prove invaluable in its role.

Two overlapping Bailey bridge sections were lashed together and placed side-by-side with two further sections. After these were braced at the pivoting end and at two points roughly halfway down each portion, with I-section steel beams, a suitably rigid bridge was created. The fulcrum point at the base of the bridge, where it met the tank's glacis plate, was braced and had an inverted U-section shaped bar system added. This secured the unit to the underside of the tank's jib when the turret was traversed, to enable the boom's cable to feed forward. This cable was then attached to a coupling, fitted to the centre of the forward-most of two supporting I-beams beneath the bridge. Secured to the shackle points at the vehicle's rear was a counterbalance framework, fashioned from steel beams and Bailey sections.

All of the details for the bridge and counterbalance mechanism varied slightly from vehicle to vehicle, as they were extemporized from available materials in the rear areas of the front. The counterbalance weights, for example, would be a mixture of concrete blocks and steel sections.

Fig. 8.22 *Note heavy weathering and discoloration to bow area.*

There were also occasions when it was desirable to tether the rear portion to a following tank, to provide stability before the bridge was dropped into place.

Even though the scratch-building of this 'conversion within a conversion' is beyond the scope of the present book, I have provided sufficient information in the form of scale drawings and illustrations to enable you to complete the project. Some further notes may also help.

Whether you use the venerable Tamiya kit or the newer Academy offering, the added weight of plastic in the form of a front-mounted bridge will demand the use of a counterweight of some sort. Though lead is the densest of materials you could apply, its use is not a great idea from the health and safety point of view. One alternative method would be the white metal used to cast model soldiers, produced by Prince August or similar.

Place the counterweight material in the rear-most section of the tank chassis until the ideal disposition is assessed, using the completed bridge at the opposite end of the vehicle. Remember, also, that the forward-most suspension bogies will be closest to the fulcrum point, at which the combined weight of the bridge and the tank will be concentrated. As a consequence, the Rock Island arsenal vertical volute suspension system of the M31 will be under terrific pressure and the swinging arms will be forced away, thus pressing the front two wheels on each side further apart. In the present day, the campaign in Iraq has shown that the suspension arms of the M1 Abrams main battle tank are prone to shearing under normal battle conditions: I have never heard of the same happening to any of the M3 or M4 variants, under the most extreme of conditions.

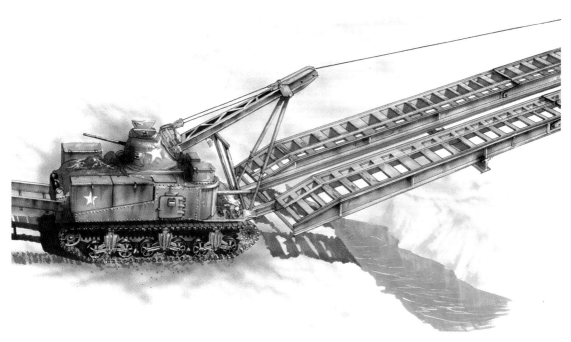

Fig. 8.23 *Assault bridge overview.*

Fig. 8.24 *Illustration showing 'T' beams in place on the underside.*

The plans and elevation drawings can be used to make templates to construct the finished bridge in the manner seen elsewhere in this chapter. The exploded view shows the final, critical construction of one of the Bailey sections in skeletal form: that is, with the tread plates removed to save weight during transportation. You can use Evergreen, Slater's or Plastruct for construction of the main bridge and attendant bracing/support portions. For the bridge sides, use 40 thou sheet with 30 thou for the 'tread'

sections. Use 5 × 2mm strip to trim the bridge sides and 10mm-deep I-section beams to support the undersides of the main structure. The final dimensions can be assessed once the scale drawings have been blown up on the photocopier, until the scale bar measures exactly 4cm. Once complete, paint should be applied via airbrush or aerosol to match the chosen colour of the main vehicle. Weathering should be heavy for a vehicle/bridge that is already in use, particularly on the roadway portion.

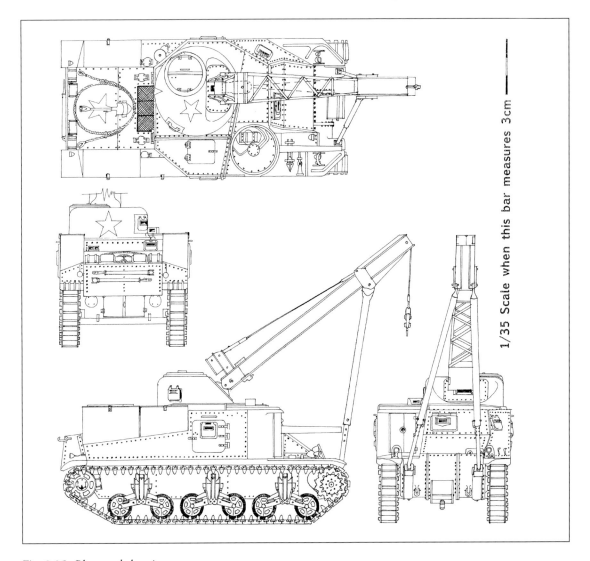

1/35 Scale when this bar measures 3cm

Fig. 8.25 *Plans and elevations.*

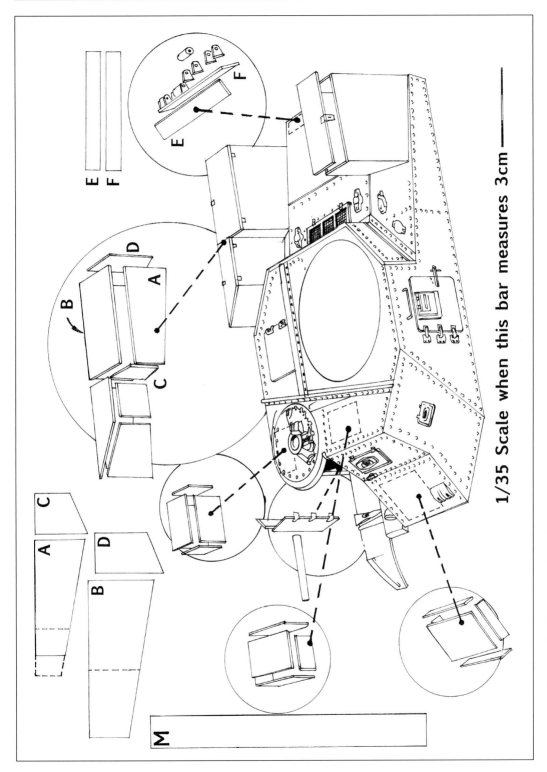

Fig. 8.26 *Hull – exploded diagram and templates.*

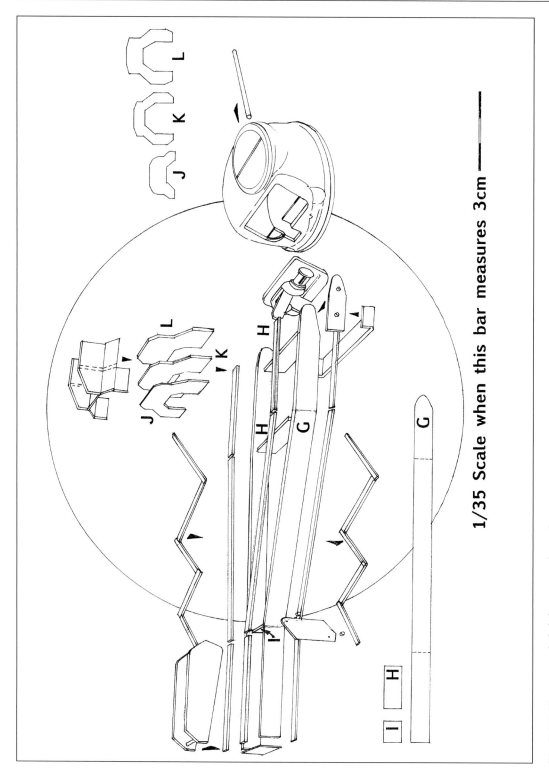

Fig. 8.27 *Turret – exploded diagram and templates.*

1/35 Scale when this bar measures 3cm

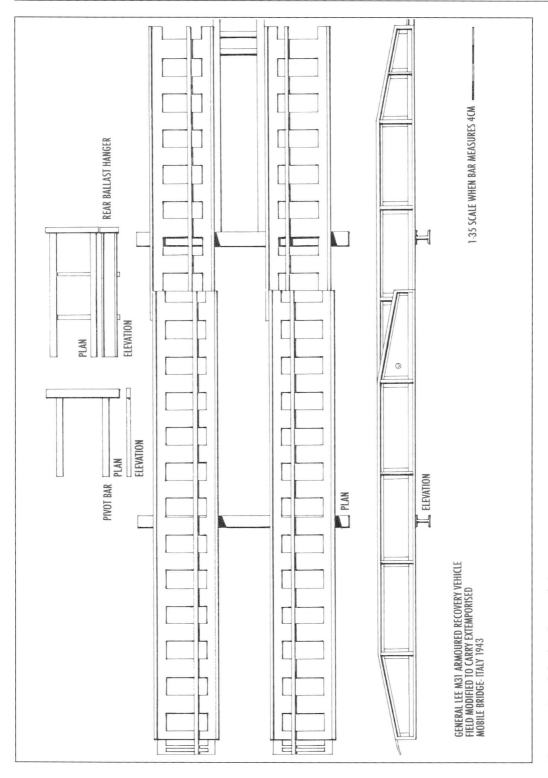

REAR BALLAST HANGER

PLAN

ELEVATION

PIVOT BAR

PLAN

ELEVATION

PLAN

PLAN

ELEVATION

1·35 SCALE WHEN BAR MEASURES 4CM

GENERAL LEE M31 ARMOURED RECOVERY VEHICLE
FIELD MODIFIED TO CARRY EXTEMPORISED
MOBILE BRIDGE- ITALY 1943

Fig. 8.28 *Assault bridge plans and elevations.*

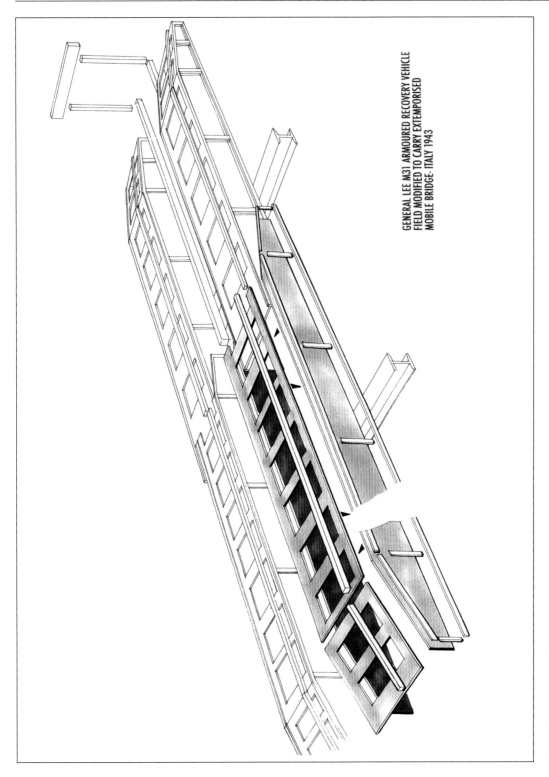

GENERAL LEE M31 ARMOURED RECOVERY VEHICLE
FIELD MODIFIED TO CARRY EXTEMPORISED
MOBILE BRIDGE- ITALY 1943

Fig. 8.29 *Assault bridge – exploded diagram.*

CHAPTER 9

Dioramas

Dioramas have been an important component of the military experience since ancient warriors drew maps in the dirt of distant battlefields. The study of battlefield topography remains a critical part of the curriculum in military academies the world over.

There are many options open to the diorama builder: some expensive, some less so. One very

Fig. 9.1 *European apartment ruin in place with plaster around.*

important consideration is size, along with the intended use of the finished item. The diorama shown here was made for photographic purposes, as opposed to being for permanent display in a house or a museum. When producing a diorama in this vein, you will need to consider the vistas and the final relationship of the buildings to the models being displayed. In the event of photography, whether indoor or on location, views should be able to be seen from a variety of angles and heights – for example, views down a street are most often from the edge of the base.

When you consider the component options available, they are many and varied, with the emphasis on quality in the main. Buildings come in all shapes and sizes, and from all ages and times. Verlinden studios recreate some stunning dwellings in plaster and resin; they all fit together easily and are reasonably priced.

I decided to depict a T-junction, somewhere on the edge of a *mittel* European town. I chose a rustic farm-building ruin and, for the opposite side of the road, part of a larger, neo-gothic apartment building (Fig. 9.1) or municipal offices. Although architectural styles such as these are often seen side-by-side in Europe, they can also act as two separate back-drops depending upon the camera angle adopted.

THE BASEBOARD

The first step is to source the baseboard. At my local timber yard I found a 70 × 70cm piece of suitably stable MDF. There are a good number of thicknesses available in both MDF and plywood. Choose a good compromise between weight and (a lack of) flexibility. I roughened and scored the surface of the MDF sheet with coarse carborundum paper, and a heavy craft knife in diagonal strokes, in order to provide a 'keying' surface to which the plaster would adhere.

To secure the trees – beech twigs – I drilled holes of a suitable, slightly undersized diameter into which I 'urged' the trunks of the trees after first dipping them into a 50–50 mix of superglue and PVA adhesive. This recipe gives a super-strong bond, along with a slight amount of 'give', in case you knock the trees during construction of the diorama. Proprietary 'Hard as Nails' glue is likewise suitable, and suits a variety of applications for the model maker and diorama builder.

BUILDINGS

The buildings were each undercoated with Humbrol aerosol enamels (Fig. 9.2), before using an ample coating of cyanoacrylate adhesive to both assemble and locate them in their allotted positions on the baseboard. Once they are securely in place, 'activator' can be used to speed up the adhesive's curing process: this must be done in a well ventilated area – preferably outside (Fig. 9.3). The road area was outlined with 5 × 5mm section wooden strips of the type used to make window mullions on large-scale doll's house projects, glued in place with superglue, then roughly plastered (Fig. 9.4).

The buildings can be given a multiplicity of textures, colours and finishes. I chose grey and dark earth in order to depict the granite and

Fig. 9.2 *Paint and weather with airbrush, before dry-brushing.*

Fig. 9.3 *Roadworks in progress.*

Fig. 9.4 *Plaster road roughly applied.*

stone types prevalent in middle Europe. Over the base coat I dry-brushed a pale stone colour: this helped accentuate any prevalent rough textures, and left the gaps where the mortar occurred in an optically darker shade of the base colour. You can add ivy or similar climbing plants to the outer side of the building, and also moss and verdigris, with tea leaves and ground, dyed sawdust over a slightly wetter than normal dry-brush coat.

GROUNDWORK

Groundwork can always be difficult to assimilate, as there is a perennial weight consideration. Many use styrofoam, or the 'oasis' foam used in the main by flower arrangers and florists – this can work out to be quite expensive. Plaster of Paris, or even hardwall plaster is an ideal method by which to cover a large area very quickly, but watch the weight of the finished product.

Once mixed to the required consistency, the plaster is best applied to the base over a network of carpet tacks, hammered into the base at irregular intervals and heights. This helps the plaster to retain its shape should any flexing of the base occur. The plaster should be applied to a minimum depth of 4mm and the carpet tacks should leave 4mm clearance below the head. Make sure that the plaster follows the contours you prefer, and that it butts up to the base of any walls and structures that you have included in your diorama.

Once the plaster is dry (usually twenty-four hours), it is time to choose the groundwork. A trip to the local model shop usually reveals a vast quantity of related items by Faller, Hornby and the like. You will inevitably end up with a suitable mix of items, most likely from different manufacturers, but don't forget domestically available products such as tea leaves for foliage on bushes and trees. Bicarbonate of soda mixed with self-raising flour can make a terrific scale snow substitute that will cover most regular surfaces – just be careful that the bicarb does not react adversely with your selected adhesive!

Once the 'sprinkles' are chosen, apply a base coat of colour to the plastered surface. You can, of course use aerosols or a 3-inch brush, along with a suitable shade of brown/green emulsion paint (matt) to suit the individual requirements.

A good trick at this stage is to add a scoop of sand or grit to the mix in order to increase and enhance the texture of the groundwork. Sprinkled grass and/or gravel can be added at this stage in a light coating, then again after it has all dried. To key the surface when dry will require the use of 3M's Spraymount or Photomount sprayed carefully onto the areas required to be grassed over. Work into all groundwork areas with various darker tones with an aerosol or airbrush in order to add areas of shadow, dampness and, where variations in soil and clay colours are to occur, often around the base of buildings and trees.

TREES

The trees are rather simple affairs: clumps of shredded lichen from the Javis model railway collection were clumped together on the branches of the previously affixed beech tree twigs. They were then given a light overspray of Spraymount and a dust-coating of railway grass. Once dry, more Spraymount and a sprinkling of dried tea leaves brought out the textures of a densely foliaged tree, its boughs heavy with both buds and leaves.

Fig. 9.5 *Excellent tree reference, which would also make a nice photographic back-drop at A3 size.*

Fig. 9.6 *Always be on the lookout for diorama references.*

This is a very simplistic tree-building method, ideal for beginners. There are, of course, a hundred different tree-building practices. Some prefer to model them using metal armatures twisted together to form a trunk, before being split into branches, the whole then being coated in plaster or car body filler and sculpted to shape. To these can then be added tiny, etched brass branches, twigs and leaves now available in maple and oak at 1/35 scale. In an application such as this, careful and planned airbrush strategy is always required.

Thinking ahead can save time and a good deal of heartache. Always collect as much reference material as possible (Figs 9.5 and 9.6). Observation is a critical pastime for model makers. When on holiday, or even whilst doing the shopping, keep an eye on the lie of the land. Take photographs of buildings and of street furniture such as forms and lamp standards in order to record variations in colour, texture and weathering. If you get the chance, check out the world wide web as well: there are a good many sites with excellent examples of the diorama builder's art: www.missinglynx.co.uk and www.totalmodel.co.uk are two in particular that I visit on a regular basis, both for information and inspiration. However, don't forget that there are new sites coming online all of the time. Finally, don't rule out the necessity to have your annual family holiday within striking distance of your chosen battlefield!

Fig. 9.7 *Halftracks in trouble.*

Fig. 9.8 *Vomag in retreat to the fatherland.*

CHAPTER 10

Panzerkampfwagen II
Ausf C *mit Schwimmkörper*

Schwimmkörper – yet another impressive German compound noun, or is it? *Schwimm* is easy, but *Körper*? This means 'body', in this case referring to the twin pontoons suspended from the sides of the vehicle. After the first few pilot models, propellers were fitted, the traction in water previously being supplied by the tracks only.

A fair few Ausf Cs were converted thus, originally for Operation *Sealion*: Hitler's planned invasion of England. When he abandoned this plan for an even more radical one – the invasion of Soviet Russia – 18th Panzer Regiment was assigned to Heeresgruppe Mitte (Army Group Centre) of the Russian front and these ugly ducklings saw extensive use in river and marsh crossings from June 1941 onward.

The engineering company of Gebr Sachsenberg in Roslau was commissioned to build these floatation devices and they were originally ready for action by October of 1940. They were certainly bulky, but with propulsion transferred from the drive sprockets direct, 10km/hr (6mph) was achievable once afloat.

PANZER II KITS

Tamiya's perennially popular Pz II first became available in the early 1970s and, in places, is unfortunately little better than a toy. It is also an Ausf F, not an Ausf C. Alongside Tamiya's new Marder III M, some of the detail is a little indistinct to say the least, though with some care and the application of a little plastic sheet, rod and strip this can make up into a very tidy and extremely cost-effective model. One of the super-detail etched sets from Aber or similar could produce some useful bits and pieces and, although not strictly necessary, could still bring this conversion in under the £20 mark. Donor parts for suspension and some superstructure work can be taken from the Tamiya Wespe kit – the tracks from this model also make a useful and more detailed replacement for the ones from the Pz II kit.

As this book goes to press, Allan of St Petersburg have just produced a wonderful kit of the PzII Ausf C. This really is a super model, with all of the detail being very crisply moulded indeed. This chapter, however, describes the conversion of the Tamiya Ausf F.

CONSTRUCTION

With reference to the plans and exploded diagrams provided, take the upper hull and a fretsaw, noting that all of the area shown within the broken lines is that which will remain of the kit part, the rest being fabricated using the template provided.

Parts T and V are the upper track guard replacements, fabricated from 40 thou sheet and inserted in the parts where surgery has occurred (Fig. 10.1). These, along with the remaining kit track guards, could always be replaced with an etched brass item if preferred.

These replacement guards had an open-weave mesh applied to their upper surface, taken from the Italeri SdKfz 234/1 to replicate the treadplate type pattern on the adjacent kit track guards. This works well once the extra rivets are in place.

Fig. 10.1 *New right fender/trackguard in place.*

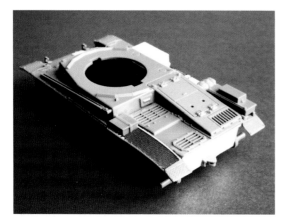

Fig. 10.2 *New rear engine plate and rear left fender.*

Fig. 10.3 *Bow and glacis plate details.*

Parts N, P, R and S, all in 20 thou strip, make up the rest of the upper hull conversion being, as they are, components of the revised fighting compartment's outer surface. Parts P and S are cemented over the void created where it has been previously cut with a fretsaw. Parts R and N are face fixed to the existing kit.

Component ZZ is the revised rear engine plate, which in the finished vehicle was bare, the engine intake and exhaust systems being housed within the structures completed in circle 1 of the exploded view. These are simple and they can be readily ascertained from the template diagram page.

Circle 2 indicates changes to turret details and requires a vice-like grip or, indeed, a vice! Drill a small hole at one corner of shaded area shown. Thread the fretsaw blade through and reaffix to its upper arm. Carefully cut around the shape shown, marked previously with an indelible pen. Trim the resultant hole and offer in part W (cut via the template from 30 thou sheet).

Components X and Y, I chose to model open: refer to the finished pictures for extra detail. The 20mm mantlet must have the existing vision slits removed and two 1.5mm plastic strip pieces re-fixed in their place, to replicate the Ausf C variant.

The pontoon brackets must now be carefully cut (two off each pattern given from 30 thou sheet) and glued in place, along with their threaded rod bracing ties, referring to all diagrams at once (part E). Once achieved, check their concurrent flatness on the underside, and their ability to marry with the pontoon's top, part A.

The pontoons are each assembled from one off parts A and B, two off part C and three off part D, which are the watertight compartment bulkheads, from 30 thou sheet. First, checking for squareness throughout, glue parts C to the edge of part A, with the latter part flat on your work surface. The adjoining components C will meet in the centre of A and need slight trimming to fit correctly.

Place the three bulkheads (part D) at the points indicated by broken lines on component A, and trim if necessary. Once they are dry, the base B can glued in place, forming the bottom of

Fig. 10.4 *Completed pontoons and body-mounted frameworks.*

Fig. 10.5 *Rear engine-plate detail.*

Fig. 10.6 *Vehicle complete without pontoons.*

Fig. 10.7 *Panzers together – standard kit, and conversion.*

Fig. 10.8 *Figure is in early war-type Panzer beret.*

Fig. 10.9 *Ready to move off.*

Fig. 10.10 *Smile please! Propaganda shot.*

Fig. 10.11 *In case of engine failure, oars were often carried.*

Fig. 10.12 *Note heavy weathering and tidemark around pontoon.*

Fig. 10.13 *Convoy crush.*

BELOW: Fig. 10.14 *Rear left three-quarter view – note the camouflage scheme.*

ABOVE: Fig. 10.15 *Overview with upper rear deck detail.* BELOW: Fig. 10.16 *Left front framework detail.*

the hull. Trim the excess edge with a craft knife once thoroughly dry.

Before mounting the pontoons to the brackets, add 5 × 3mm-diameter plastic tubes to the wheel centre of the return rollers on each side of the tank. These were there in real life to aid support of the pontoons and brace them from the tank's sides. Even now, over sixty years on, they do an admirable job in miniature.

There it is: a fairly advanced conversion and scratchbuild job with fantastic results. Super

detailing and painting I leave up to you: I used the obligatory two coats of Humbrol light sand, with 'Rot Brun' and 'Hel Grun' as random overpaints, to produce a standard 1942–3 Russian Front finish.

In the future, I plan to build a very nice (and very large) pioneer bridge in Russia in 1942. It would measure 1m in length and be 25cm+ high, carrying an 18-ton Tamiya Famo with Bilstein recovery crane conversion ... guess where the Panzer II will be!

Fig. 10.17 *The finished item.*

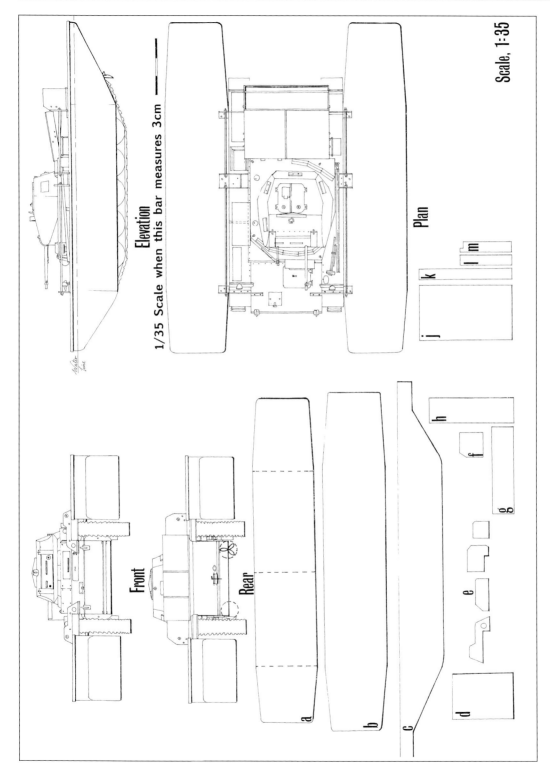

Scale, 1:35

Elevation

1/35 Scale when this bar measures 3cm

Plan

Front

Rear

Fig. 10.18 *Plans, elevations and templates.*

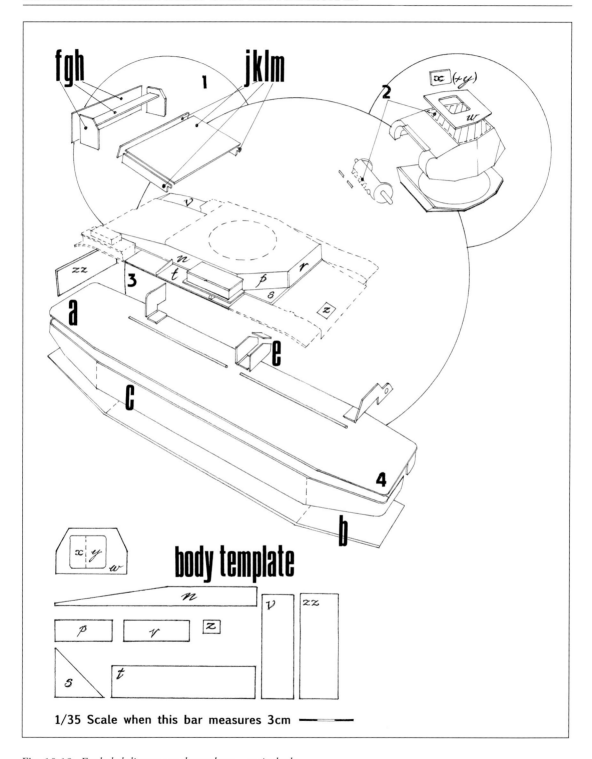

Fig. 10.19 *Exploded diagram and templates – main body.*

CHAPTER 11

Sherman Beach Armored Recovery Vehicle

The Sherman BARV was produced during 1943–44 to aid, primarily, in the recovery of tanks and their specialist derivative types used for the Normandy landings on D-Day. With the addition of a purpose-built, welded superstructure, bilge pump and deep-wading engine trunking for the exhaust and inlet manifolds, the first BARV was tested in December 1943.

Of the sixty-six produced, fifty-two were delivered in time for D-Day on 6 June 1944. Able to deep wade to 2m (6½ft), they could push or pull their charges through the surf without the need for a winch, which had been omitted in order to shorten production time. Known as the 'Sea-Lion' when it was in use immediately post-war, the Sherman BARV later gave way to the Centurion BARV, which was used up until the late 1990s by the British Royal Marines, along with their World War Two-vintage DUKWs.

Tamiya have re-engineered the moulds for their 'early production' Sherman M4 and it was used to good effect in this conversion. The extra tank crew and infantry are a real bonus for other jobs. The real tank's armour surface texture is very well reproduced and there is a great deal of excellently moulded ephemera to help line the spares box. As is so often the case with model kits of this age, there are compromises in dimensions and mould-detail but, on the whole, it makes for a model with massive conversion potential and will leave you with a spare turret! Note that if you intend to add an interior, a good deal more 'butchery' will be needed!

Fig. 11.1 *Front and rear views – the real thing.*

The donor kit needed for this conversion is the now quite venerable Tamiya M4 Sherman early production variant. During the build and once assembly of your template parts commences, you will discover not only the usefulness of the templates/exploded diagrams but also the invaluable detail content in the actual vehicle photographs included, courtesy of Ian Young.

GETTING STARTED

Complete the lower hull/running gear assembly, being careful to omit the engine rear panel and replace it with the rear bulkhead blanking plate B in the first template section using 30 thou sheet.

Carefully remove the two rear idler drivers and mountings, and replace them in the same positions at the bottom of the blanking plate (Fig. 11.2).

With the upper hull assembled (minus all of the add-on detail) mate it to the lower hull and use two off template A using 30 thou sheet to fill in the bases of the hull side sponsons, as shown in Fig. 11.5. Trim and finely sand until the fit is completely flush. Care at this stage will pay dividends, even though these parts are mainly hidden when the tracks are in place.

A small 6mm, 20 thou blanking plate can then be placed on the machine-gun bow aperture. Likewise, oval pieces to fit in place of kit parts F2 and F3 on the rear side decking can be cut using F2 as

Fig. 11.2 *Sponson infill (template A) position.*

Fig. 11.3 *Fill all redundant fixture locating holes and sand until smooth and level.*

Fig. 11.4 *Hull rear – blanking plate and lower hull rear in place.*

Fig. 11.5 *Hull rear – underside view.*

a template. Fill in all location holes for tools (spades, axes, etc.) with Milliput or similar, and sand flush (Fig. 11.3). This vehicle has very little on the exterior except the lifting lugs front and rear, plus three small angle-iron steps on the left front side (these can be added using 'evergreen' strip or similar, to the glacis plate, as shown in photographs later in the build).

HULL REAR

Components C, D and E should then be cut from 30 thou plastic sheet (Fig. 11.6). Component C should be glued into place on the hull rear as shown in the photographs. You should also check the location/angle of this piece against the scale drawings. Again, using the pictures as a guide, build up the rear bulkheads using components D and E (two off each). Take great care when adding two off template K (30 thou sheet), the superstructure/engine housing rear portions, as they may need slight trimming to mate exactly to the constructed hull rear (Fig. 11.8). They must be perfectly perpendicular, as must their forward joints with the two off parts H (30 thou sheet). When locating part H to each side (Fig. 11.10), a little filler may be needed to make a flush joint with each side of the turret-ring protector ridge, cast into the hull top.

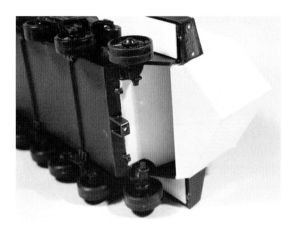

Fig. 11.6 *Fix tow-hook bracket in place as per kit instructions.*

Fig. 11.7 *Rear hull upper templates in place.*

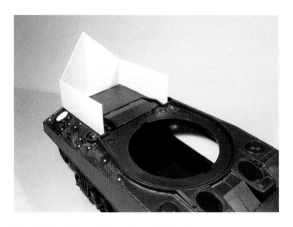

Fig. 11.8 *Two off, template 'K' in place.*

Fig. 11.9 *Check angle of rear upper hull throughout assembly.*

Fig. 11.10 *Templates 'G' and 'H' in place.*

Fig. 11.11 *Templates 'F', 'J' and 'I' in place.*

Two of template G (30 thou sheet) form the bow of the superstructure (Fig. 11.9) and should slant backwards very slightly. Again, check the angle with the main plan drawing before continuing the superstructure top.

Templates F, I and J (two off each from 30 thou sheet) provide the superstructure top (Fig. 11.11). The two F portions should be glued together along their centreline edges and allowed to dry for fifteen minutes or so before being offered into position. This method is (after some lateral thinking) a much more efficient method than one at a time. This way they are mutually supporting and provide a good way to sort out the exact angle of slope of the J template of the roof. The sectors cut from each of the two I templates are to accommodate a rectangular 9 × 14mm, 20 thou make-up piece to the rear of the venting tower amidships. A good deal of care must be taken at all stages to check for 'square' and that almost indefinable 'correct look'. Once the structure has cured completely, it will be ready to receive the conning/venting tower and rear upper housing. Whilst the central venting tower is relatively simple to construct using the dimensions from the plans and elevations, and with trimming from plastic strip, the conning tower (T, U, V, W, S and X from template) and rear upper housing (P, Q, R, M and N) take a little more time and forethought. Take care to cut

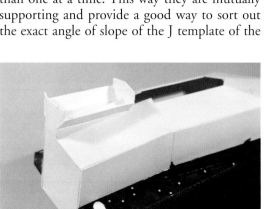

Fig. 11.12 *Templates 'M' to 'R' under construction.*

Fig. 11.13 *Positioning of conning and venting towers.*

Fig. 11.14 *Left front view with 'shadow' coating.*

each component absolutely square, yet be ready to trim edges and fill/sand as necessary.

The rear upper housing (Fig. 11.12) will require two off components N, O, P, Q and R from 30 thou sheet, whilst only one of the forward bulkhead M is needed. Again, check square throughout.

The venting tower may be modelled raised to some degree or, indeed, lowered/closed (Fig. 11.13). However, note that in the photographs of the original vehicle the centrally hinged supporting struts will therefore be in slightly different positions.

The commander's conning tower makes up into a rigid structure in its own right, even with the hatch in the open or half-open attitude (Fig. 11.14). Take great care and use a good pair of tweezers whilst adding the various hinges, hatch retaining catches and, finally, the hand rails from various fine sections of 'evergreen' strip and rod.

Exploded drawing B shows the disposition of the two off each of templates Y, Z and AA placed

Fig. 11.15 *Right rear view – note position of crew ladder (retracted).*

125

around the top edges of the upper superstructure. This shield was in place to deflect the seawater away from the exposed commander and to prevent the crew from being drenched if the main hatch was left even partially open. Each of the six template components should be carefully cut from 20 thou sheet and curved by finger/thumb pressure or by submerging in warm/hot water before being cut from the main sheet (Fig. 11.15). The outer edges should then be beaded as shown in the diagram, using a 1.5mm plastic rod.

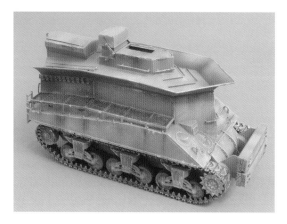

Fig. 11.16 *Front right view – weathering complete.*

Fig. 11.17 *Check relationship and positions of components throughout construction.*

The superstructure base details should then be added. The components' shapes and sizes for the driver's vision slits can again be gleaned from the plan drawings. Make up using acetate sheet (9 × 5mm), trimmed with 2mm, 20 thou plastic strip.

The two walkways are made from L-angle plastic strip for rails, cross pieces and supports (Fig. 11.16). They measure 14 × 115mm overall on the upper portion and, again, the individual support strips can be measured from the plan drawings. During their construction, try marking the exact position of the walkway on each of the superstructure sides, shown as a dotted line on diagram B. If you then cement your inboard 'angle iron' strip along this line, building the rest on is relatively simple and guarantees exact positioning of the walkway.

See the photographs for the exact position of the front 'pushing' apparatus. The side brackets are of a slightly different pattern on the plans from the type modelled here, but those are also shown in dotted line form. The radius at their bottom edge matches the curve of the outer transmission housings inboard of the drive sprockets. I used wooden strip sandwiches: four off measuring 53 × 3 × 10mm in two banks top and bottom. They would actually look quite good after grit blasting, covered in barnacles and seaweed!

Now it is time to add the detail. The mesh atop the walkways was added from that provided in the Italeri SdKfz 234 kit in two strips of 14 × 115mm in size. The angle-iron water deflectors should now be added, just forward of the 'point' of the conning tower. Tubular handrails and small hinges are components of the rear upper hull top and lead us neatly on to the rear bulkhead. With dimensions and positions gleaned from the plans and photographs, affix the hinges, catches/retaining clips, vents, bilge-draining pipes and towing hooks to and around the rear bulkhead. All of the joints on the vehicle's superstructure were seam-welded with raised, exposed residue on the surface. This can be replicated where needed by heating strip plastic with the point of a craft knife or 'pyrogravure' machine. Exercise great care at all times with strong heat sources.

PAINTING

The tracks are of the 'chevron' type (visible in Fig. 11.19), used in order to afford more traction on wet sand and shingle. They were sprayed first with a pale buff/white spirit mix, when in place around the road wheels, before dry-brushing with a silver/black mix and some suitable 'Mig' powders. Matt light grey from the Humbrol range was sprayed in two light coats over the entire vehicle. A shadowing coat was then airbrushed on with a 50–50 split of black/light grey and a liberal helping of white spirit. Dry-brushed light stone was then enhanced with a rust-coloured oil pastel to represent rust smears, then fine-brushed silver on scuffed surfaces. Remember that these vehicles were designed to withstand some very hard knocks indeed – do not be afraid to depict them!

Fig. 11.18 *M10 'Achilles' on tow somewhere in France, 1944!*

Fig. 11.19 *BARV using the front rails to push (M10 is out of gear!).*

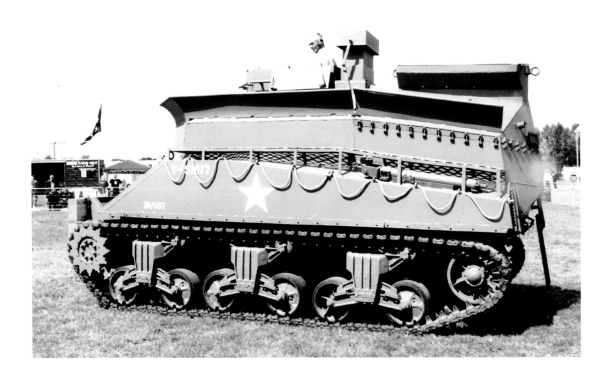

Fig. 11.20 *Full steam ahead, and with new front rails fitted.*

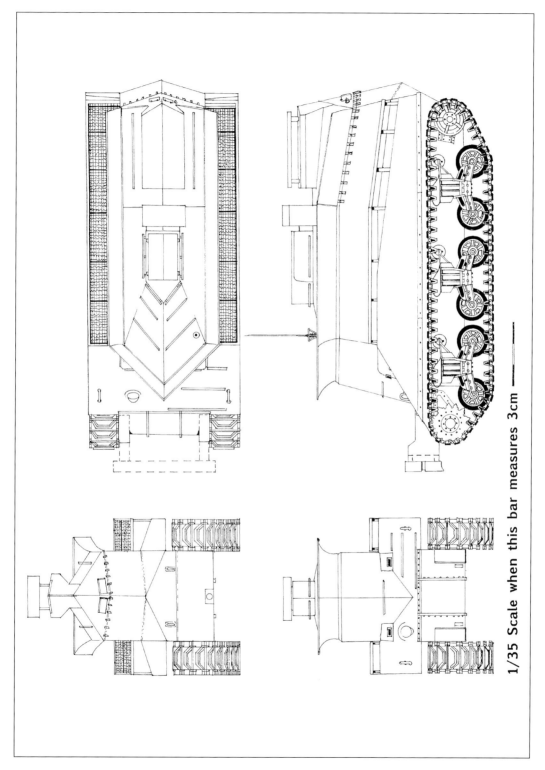

1/35 Scale when this bar measures 3cm

Fig. 11.21 Scale plans and elevations.

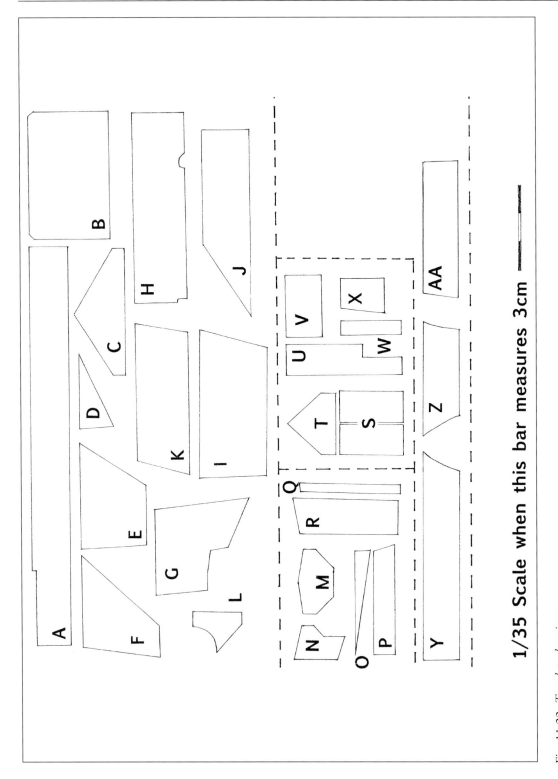

1/35 Scale when this bar measures 3cm

Fig. 11.22 *Template drawings.*

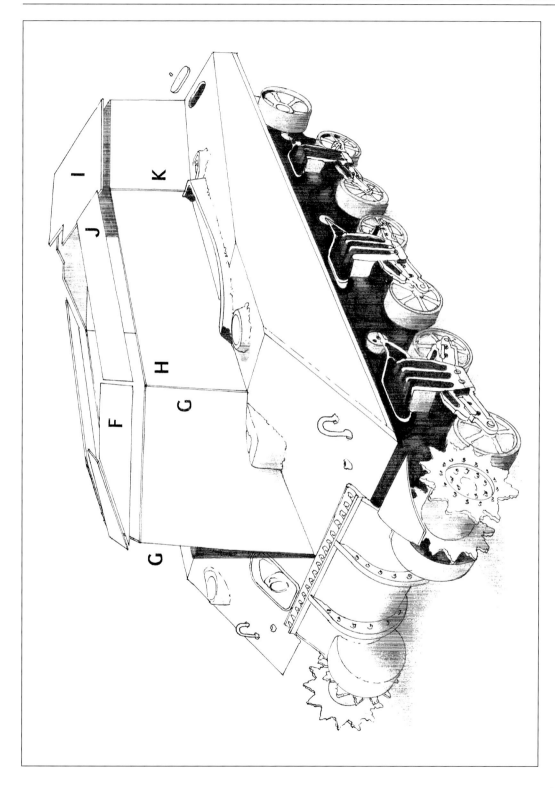

Fig. 11.23 *Exploded diagram 1.*

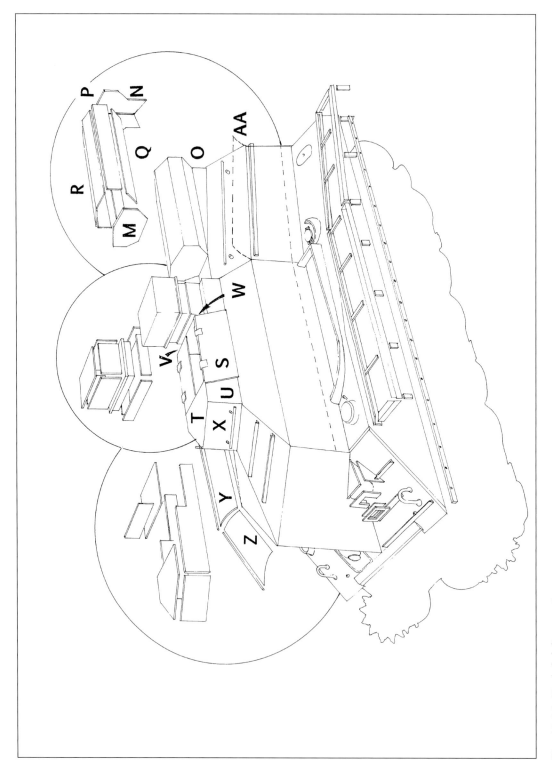

Fig. 11.24 *Exploded diagram 2.*

CHAPTER 12

BAD 2 Amphibious Armoured Car

During the 1920s, the Soviet people spent time recovering and rebuilding after the horrific experiences of the First World War and subsequent domestic revolution. The early 1930s saw the Soviet military accelerate the implementation of their new home defence strategy. The need for newly developed military vehicles to fulfil a variety of roles and have an inherently adaptable design ethos was not lost on the Soviet general staff.

Fig. 12.1 A *A tired looking BAD 2 eases into Lake Polygon.*

Most Soviet tanks of the time were eventually adapted via snorkel attachments to deep-wade the myriad of fast-moving rivers criss-crossing Russia, from its European borders to the Siberian tundra. Whilst this state of affairs was acceptable for tracked vehicles, there was a definite need for wheeled reconnaissance vehicles to have a fully amphibious capability. The BAD 2 proposal was an early attempt to fulfil this demand.

Brone Auto Drezina 2 was developed in early 1932, by N. Ya Obukhov's team at the Izhorsky plant, just outside Leningrad (now St Petersburg). Its basic layout followed that of the BAD 1, and it was the USSR's first attempt to produce a fully amphibious armoured car. Although neither it, nor any of its subsequent antecedents, entered series production, the early models were pressed into service immediately upon the outbreak of war with Germany.

From 1932 onward, BAD 2s were trialled extensively by the Red Army of workers and peasants, the RKKA. They were joined at Kazan in Tartarstan on the upper reaches of the Polygon river, by representatives of the German army general staff. These devouts were the first to witness the successes and setbacks of the BAD 2 programme. The boat-shaped appearance was no coincidence. The enclosed rear wheel arches helped reduce the turbulence produced by the propeller and increased the in-water speed to 5kt (9km/h). The main turret was fitted with a 37mm anti-tank gun; there were also two Degtyarev 7.62mm machine guns, one in the rear turret, the other adjacent to the driver's position. The front wheels, left exposed, were used as rudders for steering whilst in water but did little to help the vehicle's egress from water in any but the most ideal of circumstances.

The BAD 2's power plant was the new four-cylinder side-valve GA2 engine, which developed an excellent 40bhp. A fair proportion of this power was used up by the twin bilge pumps, which were forced into operation constantly whilst the vehicle was underway in the water: the rubber seals on the drive and propeller shafts were not sufficiently strong to completely stem the ingress of water, and were gradually replaced.

MODEL BUILD

The new Zvezda BA3 kit is an ideal model to back-engineer into its amphibious antecedent. Plastic sheet, 30 thou, is used throughout. The first step is to build the chassis and running gear exactly to the kit instructions. This portion of the construction is straightforward, with the fit of parts being decidedly 'old-school' but perfectly acceptable. The only real 'flash' problem I had was on the inner-edge of the separate tyres. I pared them carefully with a scalpel before joining to the two-piece wheel rims. These steps are amply illustrated in Figs 12.2 and 12.3.

Fig. 12.4 shows the addition of templates A and B from template page A. To position these bulkheads precisely, it is best to refer to the coloured, drawn elevation, as they are indicated as vertical lines on the hull forward and astern of the rear wheel arch. As can be seen in Fig. 12.5, the body sides and bow – template C – are offered to the chassis and assembled midships' bulkheads. The dotted lines on template C will line up with, and affix to each vertical side of, the rearmost bulkhead (A). Glue each side of the body to the vertical sides of bulkhead template B and crease slightly to achieve the bow sides' true shapes, with reference to the coloured plans. Fig. 12.6 shows the relationship of all these parts assembled.

Template K is then added to the bow, ahead of the radiator (in the manner shown in the picture) to achieve a braced, properly shaped profile, again with reference to the plan drawing. Note also that the front wheel arch inners have been cut, ready for the bracing that takes place in Fig. 12.7. Pinch the forward edge of the wheel arch inners until they are parallel to each other. Place a 30 × 5 × 2mm section of plastic strip in the place shown immediately to the rear of the engine's cylinder head. Brace with masking tape until the sub-assembly is completely dry.

Fig. 12.8 shows the assembled body with all bulkheads in place. Once completely dry, carefully bend the overhanging rear-portion sides to the shape and angle shown in the plan drawing. This rear portion can then be braced by the insertion of template E (fighting compartment floor)

Fig. 12.2 *The completed Zvezda chassis complete with engine and radiator.*

Fig. 12.3 *The rear differential and spring hangers require some trimming during assembly.*

Fig. 12.4 *Fighting compartment front and rear bulkhead assemblies.*

Fig. 12.5 *Body sides and bow in place.*

Fig. 12.6 *Clarification picture of templates' relationships, one to the other.*

Fig. 12.7 *Rear of engine bay, looking forward, with wheel-arch bracing in place.*

Fig. 12.8 *Overhead view showing forward bulkhead in front of radiator.*

Fig. 12.9 *Please note, prop shaft from gearbox to front of foremost differential yet to be added from 3mm rod.*

Fig. 12.10 *Finished forward wheel arch profile.*

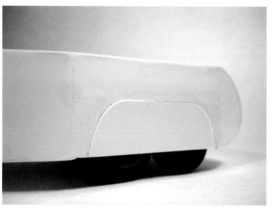

Fig. 12.11 *Rear wheel-arch cover in place.*

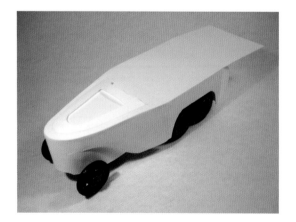

Fig. 12.12 *Hull top template in place before final shaping of rear hull.*

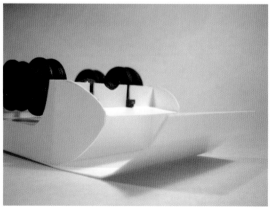

Fig. 12.13 *Hull rear top plating showing pre-creased portions.*

and F (rear floor), 13mm up from the rear wheel arch bottom edge.

After carefully cutting two off template D, these wheel-arch bottoms are cemented in the places shown in Fig. 12.9. Careful alignment with the radiused edge outermost is critical to the final bow shape – retain with masking tape until fully dry. Fig. 12.10 shows the underside of the front wheel arch assembly. A little careful trimming of the edges after completion should be enough to assure a correct bow side profile, as shown in the plans. Finish with very fine 'wet and dry' paper, as the original vehicle seems (from reference photographs) to have been fairly carefully cast, rolled and assembled, without a single rivet in sight.

Fig. 12.11 shows the rear wheel arch disposition. You can use template N, but it would be better to use the pieces originally cut when you are shaping template C at the cutting stage. Before replacing these portions, pare the edges to a 1mm depth at 45 degrees with a scalpel, to achieve their 'visual' separation in the completed assembly.

Fig. 12.12 shows template G affixed to the top of the superstructure. Note that the true shape of the rearmost portion, or 'bustle', is not yet revealed as in the template shape. I found, during assembly, that this part was better trimmed when the final bending and gluing had taken place. Template I is shown glued in place on the bow top plate. Each side of the leading edge of template G needs to be 'crimped' slightly to achieve the profile shown clearly in the plans, and secured with masking tape whilst drying.

The upturned vehicle's rear is shown in Fig. 12.13, the hull top bent carefully, in order to more readily affix to the rear of the hull sides. Retain it with tape whilst drying in order to halt the plastic sheet's natural tendency to return to its original flat form. Fig. 12.14 shows the rear underside, once the assembly has dried. If you want the hull to be watertight, fill the chassis/bulkhead slots with plastic strip. Fig. 12.15 shows template G at the rear of the vehicle being carefully trimmed (2mm strips taken off, one at a time). Always trim slowly, with the blade travelling away from you, in order to minimize the risk of injury. Fig. 12.16 indicates the finished bustle after trimming and sanding. If

Fig. 12.14 *Hull rear underside showing differential layout.*

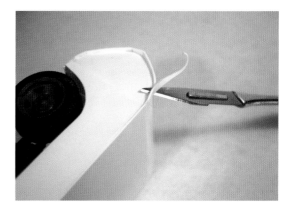

Fig. 12.15 *Trim the hull rear upper where it bends around the radiused hull sides a little at a time. Then, sand carefully.*

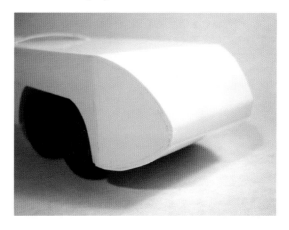

Fig. 12.16 *Rear bustle profile.*

you are careful with your template cutting and finishing, very little, or no, filler will be needed.

The exploded diagram and Fig. 12.17 amply show the disposition and fixing positions for templates J, L and M. Template J fixes to rearmost edge of template M, once it is in place below the vehicle's bow portion. It faces forward at 45 degrees to the underside plating and can be seen to good effect in the railroad illustration. Template O, the engine underside bulkhead, can now be seen in its final position to the rear of the front axle assembly – trim it to fit.

Fig. 12.18 shows the propeller tunnel, which is made from 20 thou sheet, pinched into place after a 10mm wide aperture, 15mm in length, has carefully been cut to align with the arc, cut into the bottom portion of template A. Once dry, trim the tunnel until the profile shown in Fig. 12.19 is achieved. Fill and sand if required.

In Fig. 12.20, templates T and U are shown cemented vertically on the hull top to form the central strengtheners for the driving/combat superstructure portion. It is best to brace these elements with 3mm L-section strip in order to ensure their structural strength and to make sure that the two templates remain vertical throughout the build. Note also that template I is curved to a maximum depth of 3mm at its centre.

Fig. 12.17 *Bow underside before axle scoop is added.*

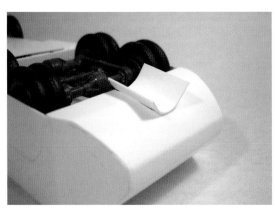

Fig. 12.18 *Propeller tunnel in place, before trimming.*

Fig. 12.19 *Propeller tunnel, final profile. The Tamiya* Schwimmwagen *will provide the propeller on a 4mm-long prop shaft.*

Fig. 12.20 *Bonnet surround profile and superstructure supports.*

In Fig. 12.21, template S is shown wrapped around the central superstructure strengtheners, as affixed in Fig. 12.20. Note that S seems to have a mind of its own and wants to spring outwards constantly! The longitudinal strengtheners linking templates T and U are 4 × 2mm strips, 25mm in length. Be prepared to hold the assembly in place until dry! Refer constantly to the plans and illustrations to ensure that the curved profile and plan for the superstructure is achieved.

In Fig. 12.22, template R, cut from 20 thou sheet, is shown atop the superstructure. Make sure to cut slightly oversized if in any doubt about your accuracy, and trim to shape once firmly in place.

Template Q is the inner windscreen portion and sits affront the superstructure at an angle corresponding to that in the colour elevation drawing.

Fig. 12.23 illustrates the state of the superstructure after the addition of components 1 and 7, which are semi-radiused around the top leading edge of template R, in order to accommodate the access hatch tower. The outer windscreen, P, is seen in place, held in part by the rear edge of bonnet template B. Its shorter edges, when bent, form the extremities of the armour portion, making the junction with the sides of template S.

Fig. 12.24 shows the hatches and their tower, manufactured from components 1–7 inclusive,

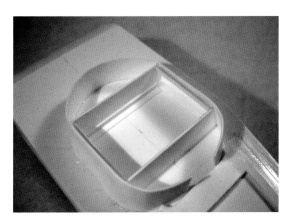

Fig. 12.21 *Superstructure wall template in place around supports.*

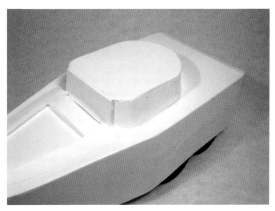

Fig. 12.22 *Superstructure top sits on top of the wall template.*

Fig. 12.23 *Addition of outer windscreen.*

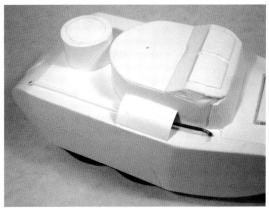

Fig. 12.24 *Rear turret assembly in place – mark the upper hull centre line in pencil.*

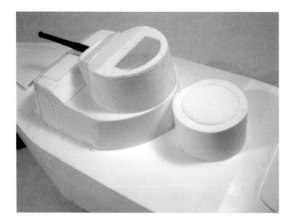

Fig. 12.25 *Relationship of turrets to superstructure top.*

Fig. 12.26 *Hull front machine gun and exhaust positions.*

Fig. 12.27 *Bow and front wheel arch profiles.*

shown in the superstructure exploded diagram. The leading edge sides (1 and 7) will need model filler and careful sanding in order to achieve the profile apparent in the elevation drawing. A 12 ×20mm piece of 20 thou sheet should be added as a cover/protector for the Zvezda BA3 kit's forward exhaust/silencer section, which is glued in the position shown. From the rear of this cover should protrude a 2 × 42mm length of plastic rod to replicate the exhaust rear section. Pinch the rear end of this where it protrudes over the top edge of the bustle, to replicate the fantail of the original's exhaust. Use templates Y, AA and Z to assemble the rear turret as shown in the superstructure exploded diagram. Use masking tape to retain template Z until the assembly is dry.

The rear left three-quarter view in Fig. 12.25 demonstrates the relationship of the main turret rear (templates V, W and X) to the rear of template R (the rear superstructure top) and template S, the superstructure surround. The turret should be fashioned in the way shown in the relevant exploded diagram, from 20 thou sheet. The 37mm main gun is added from the main Zvezda donor kit, suitably shortened using, once more, the elevation drawings as reference.

The machine gun mantlet on the front windscreen (Fig. 12.26) is taken from the Trumpeter KV2. The extra rivets were sliced from its front surface in order to back-engineer it to the earlier pattern used on the BAD 2. The vision slit covers are 4mm strips, 2 × 1mm wide, cemented carefully into the places indicated in the scale drawings. Note also the position of the bonnet inner portion from template I. It slopes upwards from the front edge to the rear by 4mm. This indicates the bonnet's position for extra cooling of the hard-working engine during the vehicle's time afloat. The main turret's hatch is glued in place. If modelled open, the hatch rests on the twin-periscopes at the angles shown. The hatch's inner handle, like the outer one on the rear turret, is taken from the donor kit, with its stem reduced to 1mm in length.

Fig. 12.27 shows the extraordinary bow shape on the bonnet's side and its relationship to the main body front. The front axle scoop (template

J) is also apparent below the bow. The optimum angle for this component seems to be 45 degrees.

In Fig. 12.28, you can see the addition of hinges (made from 2mm rod) to the two forward hatches, the main turret hatch and the offset hinge pins atop the rear wheel-arch covers. When adding the hinges it is possible, with care, to pick them up with the point of a scalpel. This aids in the accurate placing of the components immeasurably.

Fig. 12.29 is the right rear three-quarter view, showing the correct position for template H, the rear entrance hatch. Also clear in this view is the correct arching profile for the exhaust silencer guard on the vehicle's right side, amidships. The machine-gun barrel and mantlet are cut from the windscreen in the Zvezda donor kit. Fortunately, the kit's plastic is sufficiently soft to allow the mantlet to be removed from the armoured windscreen using a stout Stanley-type blade or similar.

Fig. 12.30 illustrates the forward slope of the main turret top (template X), and its exact relation to the turret surround (template V). The main gun's mantlet is carefully carved from 40 thou sheet, to 14 × 8mm. Be sure to drill an aperture to the left of the 37mm main armament, to accommodate the gunner's telescopic sight. Once the necessary filler has been added to the hatch surround, and any other joints in the hull/superstructure, a fine 'wet and dry' paper should be rubbed all over the vehicle to achieve a weld-seam free finish. In pre-war pictures of the actual BAD 2, the finish on the vehicle looks immaculately smooth with any welding/casting irregularities carefully removed before the paint was applied. When I took the model on location, I bore this in mind.

A REALISTIC SETTING

I wanted to depict the vehicle having been tested extensively, being impressed into service on the eve of World War Two. I envisaged that by this time it would have looked a little the worse for wear! The BAD 2 was tested on the Polygon river and lake at Kazan in Tartarstan. Getting a realistic location to photograph the model in could have been a problem as I don't get to Tartarstan much and

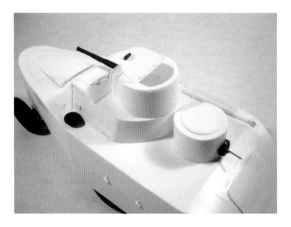

Fig. 12.28 *Main turret hatch fully open.*

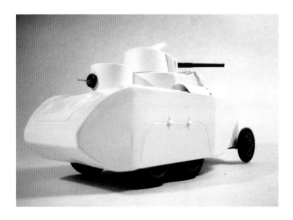

Fig. 12.29 *Rear right view shows sit of body over rear wheels.*

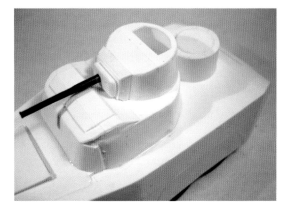

Fig. 12.30 *Note that the turret hatch is the same shape as the aperture but with a 2mm overlap all around.*

Lancashire, though picturesque, resembles Russia very little. I scanned the internet for photographs of the Tartarstan location and one particular picture of Lake Polygon closely resembles Wast Water in Cumbria's Lake District, where the location shots were therefore taken.

Fig. 12.1 shows the BAD 2 gingerly entering the Tartarstan waterway. The base coat was Humbrol's matt light olive, with various over-paints of light stone/black, and weathering applied carefully with the airbrush. The extensive rusting around the rear wheel arch and cover was achieved by sprinkling and smudging MIG powders of various rusty hues over pale stone dry-brushing before it was actually dry.

Fig. 12.31 exemplifies the BAD 2's major problem – egress from water was impossible on all but the most ideal of lightly sloped, sandy shorelines. The monochrome effect was added by my son in Adobe Photoshop and well replicates the feel of the early 1940s!

In Fig. 12.32, the Stalinetz tractor is being forced to push the momentarily disabled BAD 2 up the shingled beach. The rubber seals to the

Fig. 12.31 *Note how the bonnet star has the paint chipped from it; 20 thou sheet was used in its creation.*

engine bay and drive train were notoriously poorly made and engine misfires would have been common after prolonged waterborne trials.

In Fig. 12.33, the BAD 2 heels over by 5 degrees as she enters the shallows. Freeboard (the distance between the water's surface and the deck) was actually ample, as the BAD 2 sat fairly high in the water. The freeboard in deep water is indicated on the model by a tidemark, just above the rear wheel arch. This was applied with a pale buff airbrushed filter over a mask made from torn-edged stout paper.

Fig. 12.34 shows the BAD 2 entering the shallows and looking quite menacing. The rear lights and hatch with its handle, once more from the Trumpeter KV2, were secured with superglue as they are, like the headlights (from the donor kit), delicate. The exhaust was painted with a mixed rust colour from Humbrol pots. While wet, this was sprinkled with a relevantly coloured MIG powder to replicate a badly flaking mild steel exhaust pipe. All in all, a tricky but very rewarding conversion, that is a little off the beaten track. It will reward a slow, considered and thoughtful approach.

Fig. 12.32 *Stalinetz tractor does the hard work.*

Fig. 12.33 *The headlights are from the Zvezda kit, on 5mm rods.*

Fig. 12.34 *Rear hatch should be curved gently before fixing in place.*

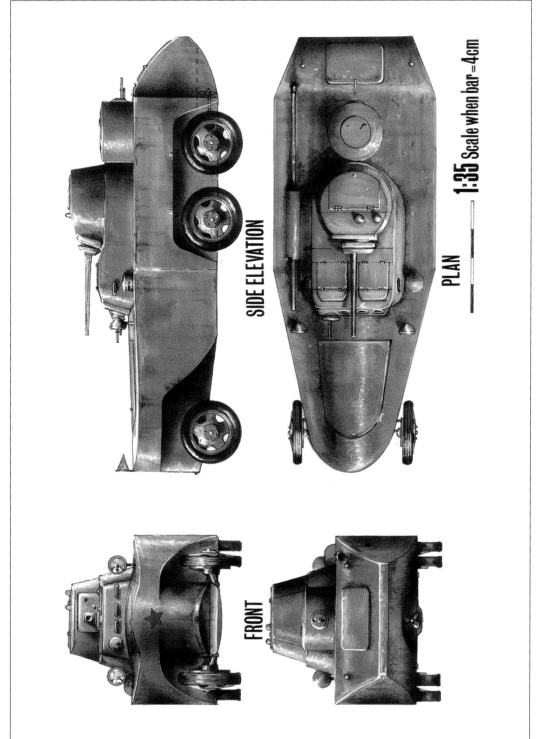

SIDE ELEVATION

PLAN

1:35 Scale when bar=4cm

FRONT

Fig. 12.35 *Coloured plans and elevations.*

Fig. 12.36 *A German officer alongside a BAD 2 (rail-equipped) – Kazan, 1932.*

Fig. 12.37 *BAD 2 on Lake Polygon showing ample freeboard.*

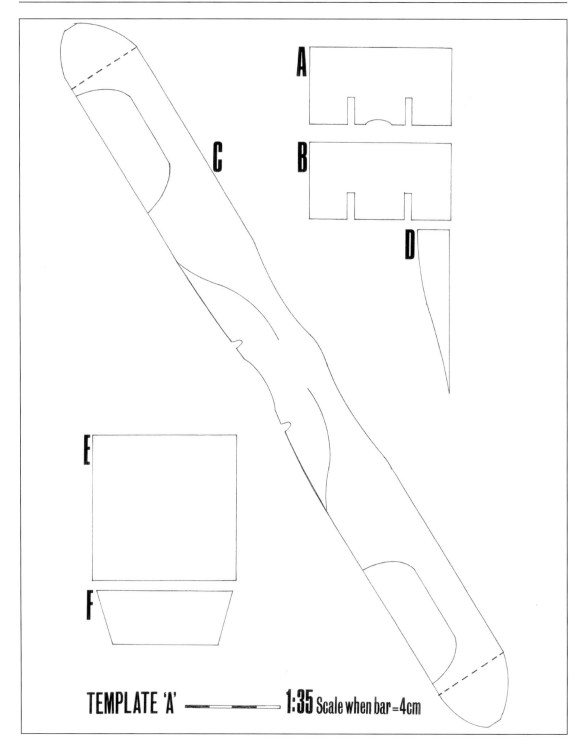

Fig. 12.38 *Template A.*

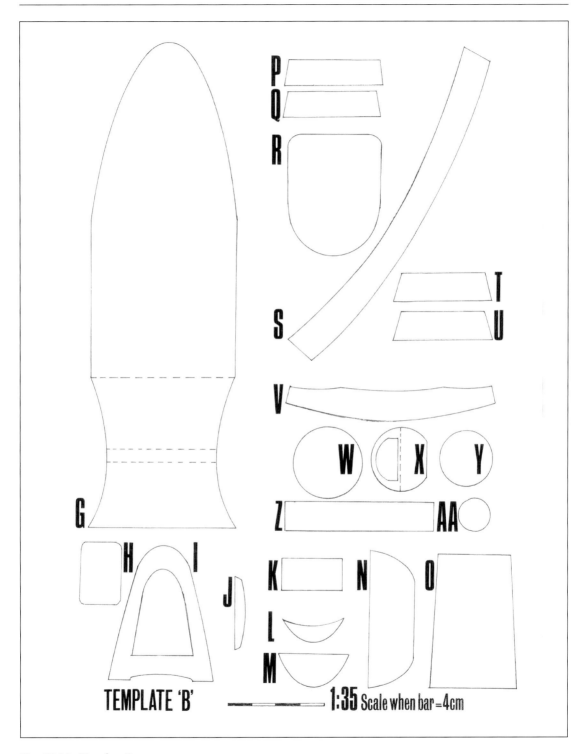

Fig. 12.39 *Template B.*

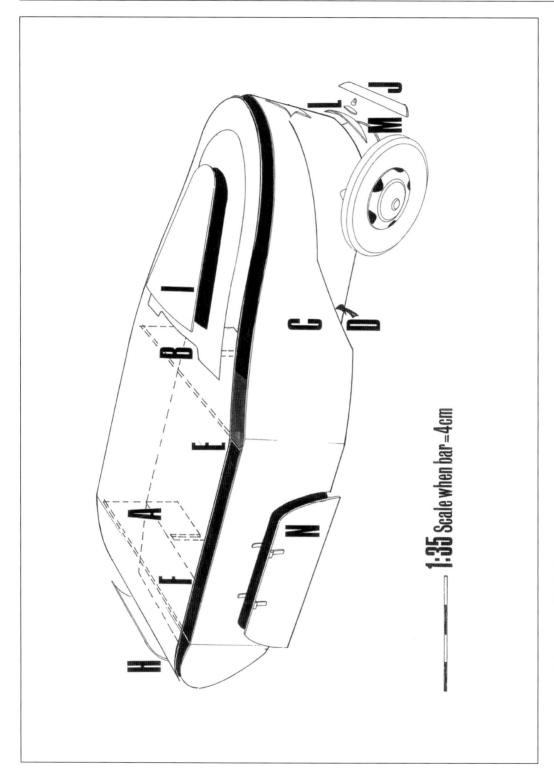

Fig. 12.40 *Exploded diagram of the bull.*

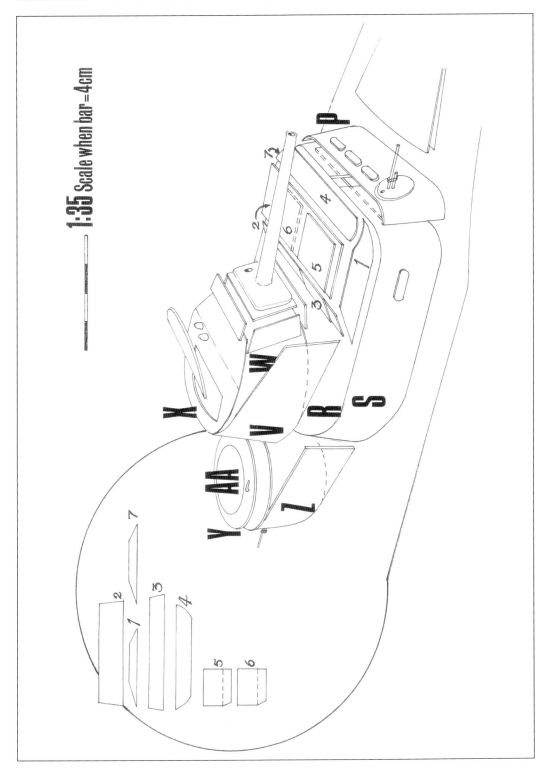

Fig. 12.41 *Exploded diagram of the superstructure and turret.*

CHAPTER 13

Vomag with 88mm Flak

In the early years of World War Two, the Germans were quick to experiment with various self-propelled mounts for their 88mm flak weapon. One type that enjoyed a good degree of success was the 9-ton Vomag bus conversion. With some judicious chassis strengthening, its low-slung floor and long wheelbase permitted the flak gun to traverse through 360 degrees and achieve its full elevation and depression. Twenty vehicles were thus converted and these provided mobile flak defence for armoured formations and cities throughout the expanding Reich.

Fig. 13.1 *88mm flak weapon, right front detail.*

Seventy-six rounds of 88mm were carried, along with signal and cable-laying equipment, to coordinate firing with other local flak units and searchlight formations. Its usual crew of eight would rapidly run out of ammunition, as two shots per minute would mean that they would be bereft after less than forty minutes of sustained fire.

Trilex wheels were included in the package which, when half-deflated, gave a fair degree of cross-country ability over soft ground. Terry at Cast-Off supplied the excellent FAMO-style wheels. Being resin items, they are beautifully detailed and the Vomag's bulged tyre bottoms (under the tremendous weight) are faithfully reproduced. The 88mm gun I used was the venerable Tamiya product. It was, and remains, an excellent model, albeit in need of a little 'super-detailing' in places. You could equally well use one of the incredible Flak 36/37 options from Dragon. The four-wheel cruciform Krupp mounting comes in handy for spare parts – especially those 'trilex'-wheels, which would look quite handsome on many wartime military transports. Excellent surface detail and textures to all parts are complemented by plastic/metal barrel options, spare shells/cases and, in some cases, an excellently sculpted crew of six storm troopers.

As we progress, other parts will be needed for springs/suspension and steering. Most of these came from any one of Italeri's large range of eight-wheeled SdKfz 234 armoured cars. The 2cm 'Hangelafette' version that I used was always an off-beat kit and one that, as so often happens with Italeri, filled a much-neglected modelling field. It has excellent, crisp detail and easy fit of parts.

This project is not necessarily as daunting as it may seem and, as long as the steps are followed carefully, a model with great strength and rigidity will result.

CONSTRUCTION

The chassis should be built using template D as a guide (Fig. 13.2). The main chassis sides and cross members are very rigid once glued together in the correct sequence. Use 5 × 3mm plastic rod

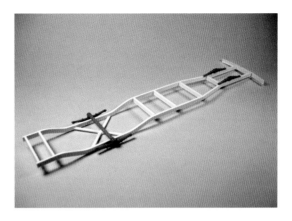

Fig. 13.2 *Note side-rail 'kinks' to chassis, and rear spring hanger bar in centre of 'X' cross member.*

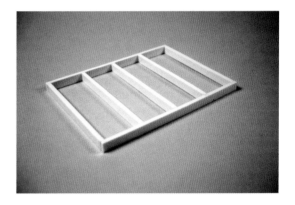

Fig. 13.3 *Template 'A' – gun platform cradle, complete.*

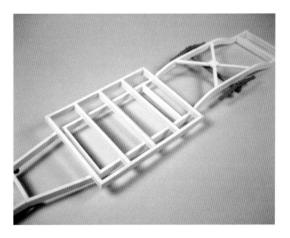

Fig. 13.4 *Gun platform cradle in position with rear edge at bottom of side rail's forward slope.*

(rectangular section) and, if necessary, tape this lightly over your copy of the drawing to ensure squareness and accuracy during assembly. After cutting each component, ensure squareness of the cut with the judicious use of fine emery paper on a flat surface.

The kink in the rear portion, which accommodates the rear axle assembly, can be achieved by careful bending, using finger and thumb. However, you may like to try immersing the rod in warm water (as warm as you can stand) then bending around a former made from softwood with wire nails in the correct places, relative to the side elevation in the template drawings. During the build, constant reference should be made to the scale drawings, templates and relevant photographs, to cross-check information when necessary.

The X-shaped cross-member requires careful construction, the angles being checked constantly to ensure squareness. The pieces' integrity will be greatly increased by the addition of the 'squaring' plate shown at its centre, cut from 30 thou sheet.

Referring once more to the plan and pictures, join the front and rear springs from Italeri's SdKfz 234 kit to the completed ladder chassis. The rear springs are joined latitudinally by a 42mm length of trimmed sprue from the kit, which glues directly to the chassis outer legs. The front springs locate via shackles, 5 × 2mm (eight

off), to the forward end. Check exactly on the plan drawings.

Template component A is constructed in the same manner as the chassis (Figs 13.3 and 13.4), but from 4 × 5mm plastic bar. The location is shown precisely in the photographs at the bottom of the chassis' rear forward slope. Check for squareness throughout the construction sequence and, if necessary, trim accordingly. Mark the chassis and the completed component A with a pencil when they are in precisely the correct position. Use these marks as a reference point whilst the glue is curing. If needed, the parts can be held together momentarily with masking tape.

Prepare the next batch of parts – the wheels and running gear – using plans and pictures as reference. The wheels from Cast-Off (Fig. 13.5) require a little work with the Dremel to remove the remains of casting lugs and minimal flash. The brake drums for the inner portion of the Trilex hub are simple 12mm diameter, 30 thou discs: two to each wheel, making a 60 thou sandwich to replicate each part. These, once cut with a circle cutter, should be carefully glued with cyanoacrylate adhesive to the centre of the hub rear. For the four rear wheels, an 8mm disc must be made from 20 thou sheet for each of the wheel centres. A 2.5mm hole in each centre will ensure that it fits over the central hub nut on the wheel's outer face.

Fig. 13.5 *Two halves of brake drums mounted centrally in wheel rear.*

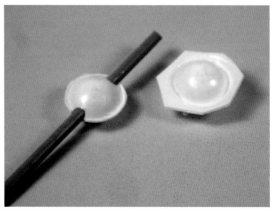

Fig. 13.6 *Differentials under construction on sprue axles.*

The rear axles measure 57mm in length each and are made from Italeri's sprue (Fig. 13.6), with differentials added as shown in the pictures. The differentials are each made from 2 × 15mm domes plastic sheet bowls. I used an old camera filter holder and a glass marble as male and female formers, pressing one into the other with a 30 thou sheet of plastic card in between; the card had first been heated under an electric grill. It takes practice, split-second timing and, at the end of the day, is not recommended! Health and safety are paramount and suitable differentials and axles can easily be sourced from other kits before being thus converted.

Examine the wheels carefully, to establish where the 'bulges' occur, as these should be lowermost when glued to the axle ends, and flat spots (Figs 13.7–13.10) should be sanded or ground where the tyre bottom meets the ground. A much more realistic look is achieved by this method, bearing in mind the weight of the truck and the 88mm gun.

The 'dead-beam' front axle (Figs 13.11 and 13.12) can either be scratchbuilt using the template next to D or, once more, cannibalized and extended from any of the multiplicity of German truck kits available.

The steering tie-rods shown in the photographs are once more from the Italeri armoured

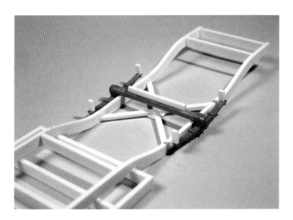

Fig. 13.7 *Axle hanger blocks in place, with central latitudinal anchor point for inboard 'half-spring'.*

Fig. 13.8 *Rear wheels in place – make sure that they are square to the chassis whilst the glue is drying.*

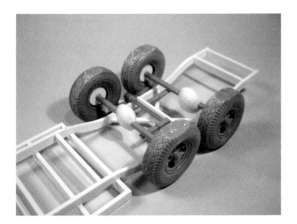

Fig. 13.9 *Half-springs in place between axle tops and central latitudinal anchor point.*

Fig. 13.10 *Note 'flats' on tyre bottoms – best done with coarse, then fine wet-and-dry paper.*

car. Please note, when adding these, that the German 'Ackermann' centre-point steering system applies, hence the end of each tie-rod facing rearward would, if you traced an imaginary line to the rear of the vehicle, meet at a point in the centre of the forward-most rear axle. Referring to the photographs (Fig. 13.13) once more, you will note the disposition of the propeller shafts running under the centre cradle (4) into the differential axlebulges, with their offset castings added from Milliput. Their flanges (with bolt heads) are again from Italeri's 234 kit, secured with superglue.

Next, the air-braking system twin reservoirs and their attendant piping are added (Fig. 13.14), running from the engine power take-off to the reservoirs and on to flexible pipes to each wheel hub. Reference for these is scant, so, good luck! On the chassis' opposing leg is the exhaust silencer (*see* Fig. 13.14) made with 1.5mm plastic tube, which runs forward to the engine exhaust manifold and at the other end appears on the offside amidships.

The main gun platform, which sits on the top of cradle A (Figs 13.15–13.18), is cut carefully and trimmed using template B. Use 40 thou plastic sheet, as this will faithfully replicate the scale thickness of the original and adds a good degree of much-needed rigidity at this stage of

Fig. 13.11 *'Dead-beam' axle and 'tie-rod' in place on front springs.*

Fig. 13.12 *Brake slave-cylinder in place on reverse of front hub.*

Fig. 13.13 *Exhaust, silencer and rear prop-shaft positions.*

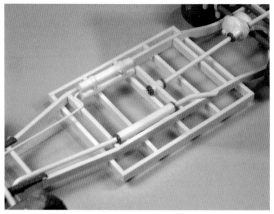

Fig. 13.14 *Twin cylinder brake air reservoirs with 'plumbing' to the engine power take-off.*

Fig. 13.15 *Spring shackles. Let dry as shown before securing opposite end.*

Fig. 13.16 *Gun platform, template B mated to gun cradle.*

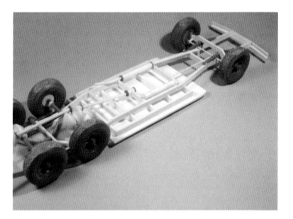

Fig. 13.17 *Gun platform underside showing its relation to template A, the gun cradle.*

Fig. 13.18 *Spring shackles secured to opposite end, around the rear axle. Sand the filler on the 'diffs' until smooth.*

the build. For the exact positioning, refer to the scale plans.

To complete the rear ammunition stowage locker (Figs 13.19–13.25), refer to the exploded diagram. Cut out templates G (locker sides, two off), I and J (locker top sheets), S (seat back), T (locker bottom rear) and U (locker bottom) from 30 thou sheet. As shown in the photograph, several other pieces – seven in all – will be needed to complete the wheel arches. These are easily measured and constructed (all in 30 thou sheet) once the sub-assembly is completed and offered to the chassis. Note that locker stowage doors in parts G and rear body plate Z will need to be pre-cut

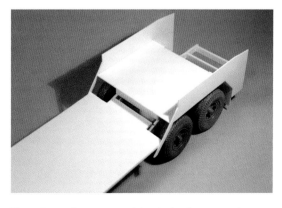

Fig. 13.19 *Rear ammunition locker housing sides.*

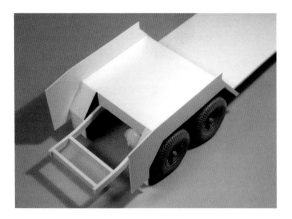

Fig. 13.20 *Position of inner rear wheel-arch panels. Note 'diff' bleed screw below.*

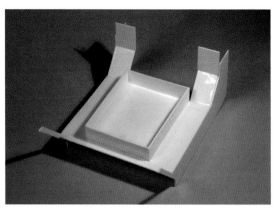

Fig. 13.21 *Underside 'cradle' of rear ammunition locker housing.*

Fig. 13.22 *Relationship of templates T and I, positioned so that template Z will be vertical.*

Fig. 13.23 *Position of fuel filler-cap inner from 7mm tube cut at 60 degrees.*

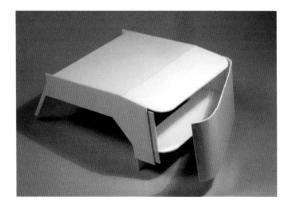

Fig. 13.24 *Template Z showing retaining tab to aid jointing.*

Fig. 13.25 *Ammunition locker doors in place – note rounded edges top and bottom.*

before assembly if the relevant doors (shown dotted on the templates) are to be modelled open. The affixing of component Z is shown on the photograph. The curved ends were achieved by careful hand bending of the 30 thou sheet. The location strip shown on the rear edge of part G is a prerequisite. After careful measuring and joining at this juncture, set the assembly to dry thoroughly before sanding and blending the resulting join.

Once the stowage locker is mated to the chassis rear (Fig. 13.26), the doors, hinges and locks can be added. Also, note that the petrol tank filler cap recess is only apparent on the right-hand side panel. The seat slabs, as with the forward ones, were carefully fashioned and 'mis-treated' using 60 thou sheet. This, I find, is best scored and 'snapped' using a heavy craft knife.

The front wheel arches are fashioned as per Figs 13.27–13.29, using templates AA (two off), BB (four off) and six off 19mm strengthener strips. For each side, once two off template BB have been affixed opposite each other using the strengthener strips, a length of 20 thou sheet, 20 × 55mm, is hand curved, then affixed around the assembly. Whilst holding in shape with low-tack masking tape, part AA – the wheel arch rear – can be glued in place. Leave this whole to dry for twenty-four hours. When affixed to the chassis legs, any springing can be contained using front and rear supports, as shown in the photographs.

Fig. 13.26 *Relation of forward wheel arch slope before trimming level with bottom edge of gun platform.*

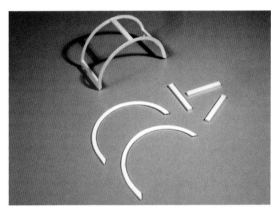

Fig. 13.27 *Templates BB with spacers.*

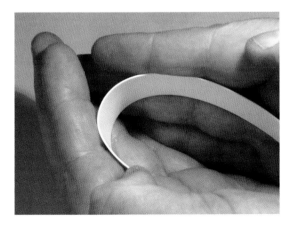

Fig. 13.28 *The heat generated when rolling your wheel-arch outers will help them retain their final shape.*

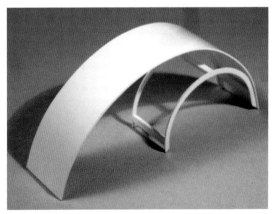

Fig. 13.29 *Wheel arch skin. Leave to dry at one end before securing the other.*

Fig. 13.30 *This shows how the arches can spring outward before the crew-steps and front bracings are added.*

Fig. 13.31 *Template E in place, note exhaust pipe front end below it.*

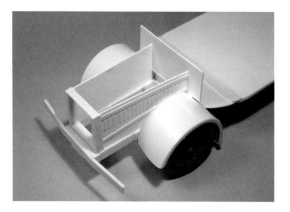

Fig. 13.32 *Bonnet sides, with louvres, and stamped strengtheners in place.*

For exact size and position, refer to the scale plans. Glue in position driving compartment floor C and engine firewall E cut from 30 thou sheet (Figs 13.30 and 13.31). Also note from the photographs at this stage that there is a small radius sanded to each outer edge of the wheel arches. Check throughout that all parts remain square.

The bonnet sides (Fig. 13.32), template K (two off from 30 thou sheet), are cemented in place atop the forward chassis rails. All detail must be added before assembly, using the plans as a guide. These 'sides' are not placed parallel on the chassis: they must align with its inner edge at the bonnet front.

The radiator is not actually behind a grill, it is an exposed series of vertically fluted 'veins'. Once the radiator surround is in place, a 19 × 23mm 20 thou sheet forms the radiator core with 1mm diameter rod (eight off) to form the veins.

The bonnet top, H (Fig. 13.33), and its formers – L (rear), M (centre) and N (front – exposed) – are then cut from 30 thou sheet. The curve follows these formers exactly and the whole assembly – with longitudinal strengtheners – should be left to dry for twenty-four hours, with masking tape used as a retainer. Former L, when complete, should butt up to engine firewall E, making a sound, square component. Former N should protrude over the radiator surround top, being a close, flush fit. The inside of the firewall then needs template P and two upright strips, as per the photographs, to form the dashboard.

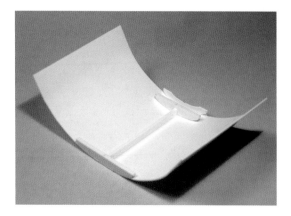

Fig. 13.33 *Underside of 'anti-strafing' bonnet cover, showing formers in place.*

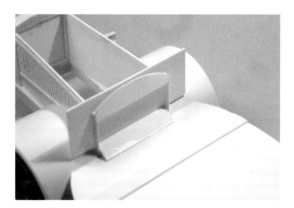

Fig. 13.34 *Dashboard and side supports in place.*

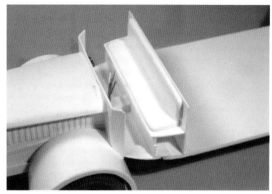

Fig. 13.35 *Sixty thou seat slabs centrally in place.*

Fig. 13.36 *Bonnet cover, doors and door-hinges secured.*

Fig. 13.37 *Position of steering wheel and bonnet side handles.*

Once template F (driving compartment rear wall, Fig. 13.34) is in place, doors X and Y (two off each, Fig. 13.36), along with door pillars, should all be glued using the plans to carefully establish their exact positions. The front doors, X, are both sloped forward on their top edge and curved to align with the side-shapes of component C. Seat slabs, infill parts, foot pedals and brake/gear stick positions can all be seen in the photographs (Figs 13.35 and 13.37), the latter being cannibalized from the Italeri armoured car kit. The seat slabs are made from 60 thou sheet and the steering wheel comes from Tamiya's FAMO, but all of these extra parts can also be scratch-built or sourced from the many after-market makers.

Checking for squareness throughout assembly is critical. Door Y's top must be in an exact line

with G's top (Figs 13.38 and 13.39), to ensure that the fighting compartment sides – built from 1.5mm strip using templates V and W – align exactly. As throughout, some trimming of components may be necessary but will pay dividends. Also, at this stage, always refer to your plans and reference shots in order to add the necessary details.

Careful assembly of template V will be necessary. The 'netting' to its inner face comes from the Italeri kit and glues neatly in place with plastic model glue. The struts and hinged plates were then added; their seating is on cradle A's outer edge, in the places shown in the relevant photograph.

The front windscreen measures 50 × 18mm outside dimension and is formed from small

Fig. 13.38 *Templates V and W should complete the straight line atop parts Y and G.*

Fig. 13.39 *Note extra bar and central retainer atop the windscreen.*

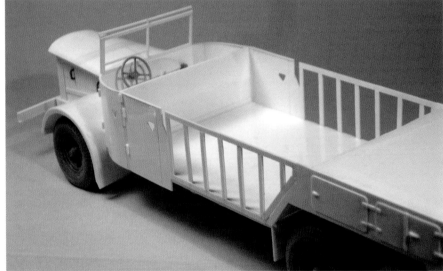

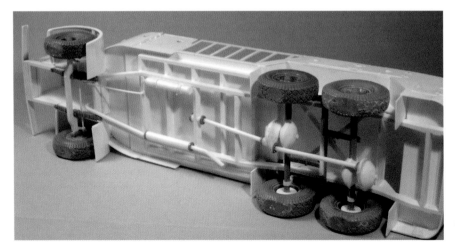

Fig. 13.40 *Underside showing position of 'reduction' differential housings.*

L-angle plastic strip and rod; likewise the wiper and sun-screens. All other details, such as the bumper, wheel arch struts, sidelights, hinges, door handles and so on, can be clearly seen in the photographs and plans. Judgement needs to be used as to the best method of manufacture for yourself.

Atop compartment J sits the wire frame for the canvas tilt and the metal-rod enclosure for crew kit and canvasses. These are clearly shown in the plans and can be readily put together using 1mm-diameter plastic rod.

The front and rear jacks are made from plastic tubing strip: exact sizes and dimensions for the rod can be gleaned from the drawings; likewise with the telescoping side-jack/supports. These fold amidships forward, against the chassis sides,

and are partially hidden by two hinged panels (10 × 36mm), shown carrying spades. Their exact size can be ascertained from the plans.

I added headlights/convoy light from the Tamiya SdKfz 222. The driver's front step and its opposing duplicate can be cut from the Italeri armoured car fighting compartment floor, suitably trimmed and thinned.

Made from 2mm strip, the rear wheel-arch surrounds are added (Fig. 13.46) and any final hinges, seats, door locks, and so on, put in place before the 88mm mounting is affixed to component B using the cross-hairs as a sighting guide.

Any of the 88mm flak guns made by the major manufacturers will be eminently suitable. The spares box and your stowage for this model will

Fig. 13.41 *Hinge details attaching template V uprights to the gun cradle frame.*

Fig. 13.42 *Trunnions and gudgeon-pin detail to front hubs, and positioning of crew-step bracing bracket.*

Fig. 13.43 *Cable drum positions on rear of hull.*

Fig. 13.44 *Fighting compartment forward outer crew seats – undersides.*

Fig. 13.45 *Completed model before painting. Note Panzer grey undercoat on 88mm flak gun.*

Fig. 13.46 *Please note position of rear number plate and light.*

Fig. 13.47 *Rear wheel-arch detail before trimming and sanding.*

Fig. 13.48 *Vomag logo under construction.*

also benefit – ammo boxes will help stow the Vomag and any ancillary ammunition vehicle you may deem fit. Remember to fit the prismatic, tubular sighting device and affix the cable reels with their mountings to the rear of component Z.

These vehicles were originally painted in Panzer grey, but as the war progressed so did they – into the three-colour scheme shown here and also seen in photographs taken around Magdeburg in 1943. My vehicle is well worn and shows paint (often of inferior quality), which is chipped in places, to show through the original factory-applied finish.

Fig. 13.49 *Vomag logo complete, forward jack detail and position of 'Notek' light.*

Fig. 13.50 *Radiator close up – note scratches revealing 'Panzer grey' undercoat.*

Fig. 13.51 *Front left view – note the weathering.*

Fig. 13.52 *Rear right view.*

Fig. 13.53
*Alternative radiator
logo.*

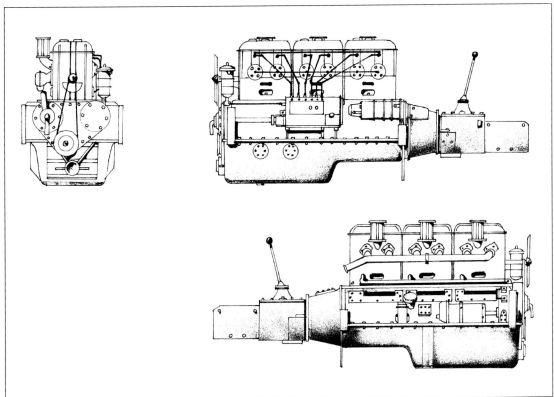

Fig. 13.54 *Engine plans and elevations.*

Fig. 13.55 *'Magdeburg' camouflage with tarpaulin-covered main armament.*

Fig. 13.56 *Standard 88mm weapon – Johannesburg war museum.*

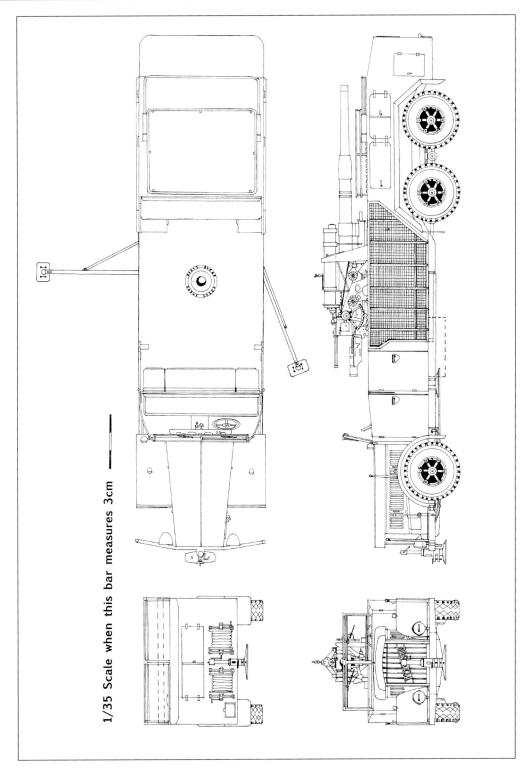

1/35 Scale when this bar measures 3cm

Fig. 13.57 *Plans and elevations.*

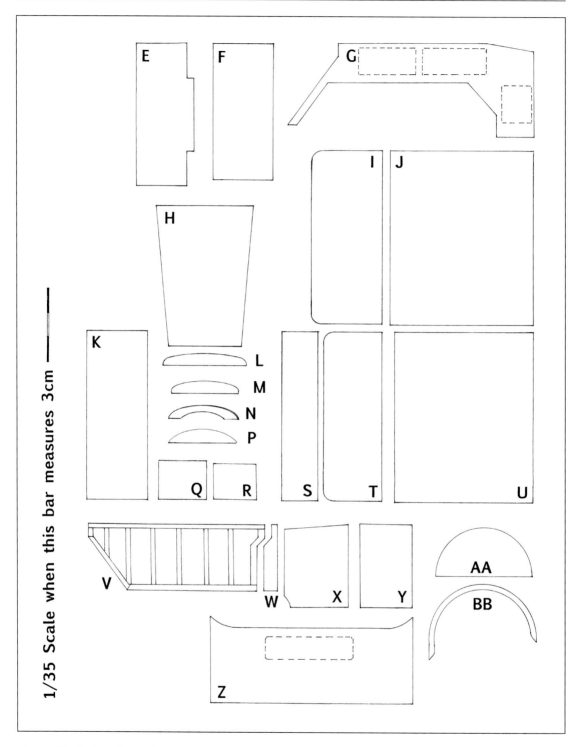

Fig. 13.58 *Bodywork template.*

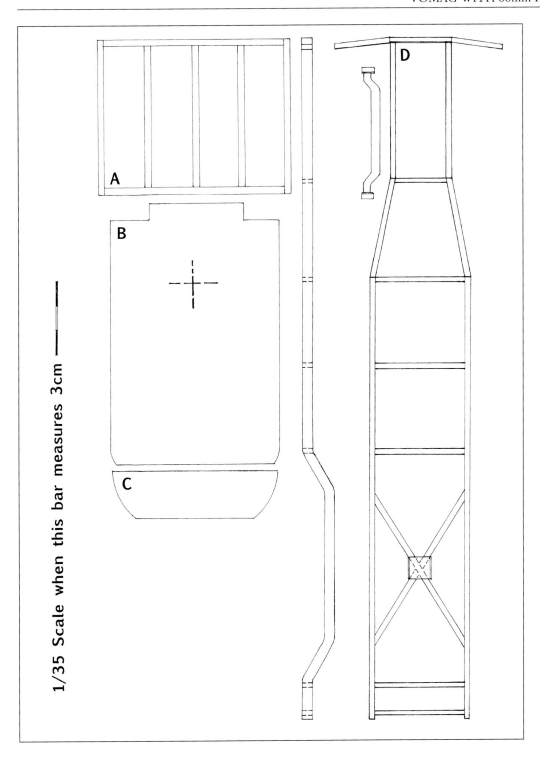

Fig. 13.59 *Template 2.*

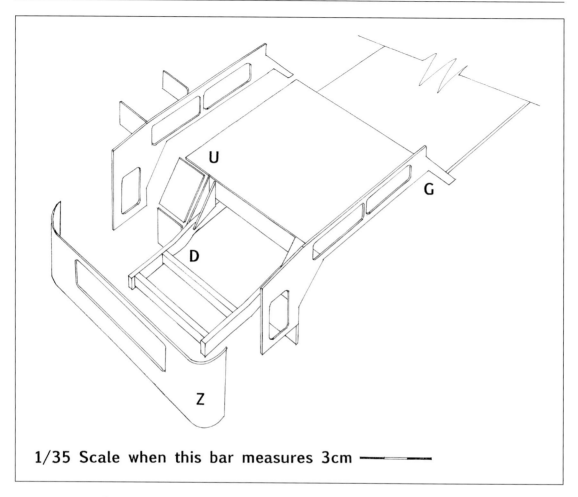

1/35 Scale when this bar measures 3cm ▬▬▬▬

Fig. 13.60 *Assembly diagram – rear body.*

Bibliography and Useful Websites

Bean, Tim and Flowler, Will, *Russian Tanks of WW2*. ISBN: 0-7110-2898-2

Blackman, John, *World War 2 Military Vehicles*. ISBN: 0-7110-2330-1

Chamberlain, Peter and Ellis, Chris, *British and American Tanks of World War Two*. ISBN: 1-84509-009-8

Chamberlain, Peter and Doyle, Hilary, *Encyclopedia of German Tanks of World War Two*. ISBN: 1-85409-518-8

Crow, Duncan (ed.), *Armoured Vehicles of Germany*. ISBN: 0-214- 20307-7

Fowler, Will, *Jeep Goes to War*. ISBN: 1-56138-235-3

Frank, Rheinhard, *Trucks of the Wehrmacht*. ISBN: 0-88740-686-6

Gander, Terry, *Medium Tank M3 to M3A5*. ISBN: 0-7110-2983-0

Georgano, G.N., *World War Two Military Vehicles – Transport and Halftracks*. ISBN: 1-85532-406-7

Kliment, C.K. and Doyle, H.L., *PzKpfw 38t in Action*. ISBN: 0-89747-089-3

Sowodny, Michael, *German Armoured Rarities 1935–45*. ISBN: 0-7643-0396-1

Vanderveen, Bart, *Historic Military Vehicles*. ISBN: 0900913-57-6

Wise, Terence, *D-Day to Berlin*. ISBN: 1-85409-212-X

Zaloga, Steven, *US Armored Artillery in World War Two*. ISBN: 962-361-688-0

Zaloga, Steve and Sarson, Peter, *M3 Infantry Halftrack 1940–73*. ISBN: 1-85532-467-9

MAGAZINES

Classic Military Vehicles (ed. by Pat Ware). Published by Kelsey Publishing Group.

Military Machines (ed. Ian Young). Published by Model Activity Press.

Tamiya Model Magazine (ed. Marcus Nicholls). Published by ADH Publishing.

Wheels and Tracks (ed. Bart Vanderveen). Published by Kelsey Publishing Group.

USEFUL WEBSITES

www.cobbatoncombat.co.uk
www.friendsoftheforties.co.uk
www.hmkf.no
www.jeepworld.co.uk
www.modelactivitypress.co.uk
www.mvt.org.uk
www.orbmilitary.co.uk
For Vomag wheels, email castoff@castoff.karoo.co.uk

Index